The Theo Workb

CW00538478

This workbook has been developed in association with the *Driving Standards Agency* the people who set and control the actual theory and practical driving tests.

Published by: Teaching Driving Limited
(01977 600458)

Version: *1998/99 valid until August 1999*

ISBN: 0-9529035-2-0

Compiled and written by: Aeneas MacRitchie (ex. DSA supervising examiner) and Paul McArdle

Graphic Design by: Michael Bedford

Origination: Design and layout computer generated using "CorelDRAW and Pagemaker"

Printers: George Over Limited

© Copyright:
Crown copyright material reproduced under licence from the controller of HMSO and the *Driving Standards Agency*.

The question programme forms part of the:

LEARNER DRIVING SYSTEM

Questions, answers and images supplied by:

DRIVING STANDARDS AGENCY

Contents

Overview

This workbook provides you with the ideal way to learn the knowledge you need to pass the theory test for cars. It provides a comprehensive training plan for you to follow that can be combined with your practical in-car training and your study of the Highway Code. This means that as you learn the theory you can apply it in practice. Naturally, this makes the theory much easier to learn as it becomes part of the natural process of learning to drive.

A structured learning programme

The theory test programme detailed in this workbook will take you through the full data bank of official DSA theory test questions for cars (i.e. 878 questions in total) in a logical learning sequence. So, for example, all the questions relating to pedestrian crossings are grouped together so that you can learn the theory and then apply it in practice on the pedestrian crossings driving lesson. In all the other books currently available these same questions would be spread over several different headings (i.e. Road & traffic signs, Rules of the road, Attitude, Hazard awareness, Vulnerable road users etc) making it far more difficult to learn. Consequently, we have taken all the official DSA theory test questions for cars and restructured them, such that they form part of a properly structured training programme - The Learner Driving training programme.

The Learner Driving training programme

The theory lessons in this workbook go hand-in-hand with practical driving lessons. They combine to form the Learner Driving training programme. Although the theory goes hand-in-hand with practical driving lessons you do not need to undertake the practical lessons if you are solely interested in passing the theory test at this stage. The programme is still very effective standalone.

To help you appreciate how the theory lessons link with your driving lessons we have shown the Learner Driving practical programme of driving lessons overleaf.

Practical driving lessons:

Part 1 - Basic control skills:
1. Getting moving
2. Gears
3. Steering
4. Co-ordination
5. The emergency stop

Part 2 - Road skills:
6. Hazard drill and approaching junctions
7. Emerging from T and Y Junctions
8. Crossroads
9. Roundabouts
10. Traffic signals and pedestrian crossings

Part 3 - Traffic skills:
11. Defensive driving and perception
12. Dual carriageways
13. Town and city centre driving
14. Progressive driving
15. The driving test

Set Manoeuvres:
M1	Straight line reversing
M2	Reversing to the left
M3	Reversing to the right
M4	Turn in the road
M5	Reverse parking

To help you prepare for each practical driving lesson in the Learner Driving programme we have also produced a comprehensive video and workbook package. The workbook is entitled "The Driving Skills Workbook" and the video is entitled "The Driving Skills Video".

These materials are designed to direct your practical training and help you understand the underlying principles and procedures associated with the skills you will need to master on each lesson. To help illustrate key points during the driving lesson there is also a laminated colour presenter that can be used with dry marker pens.

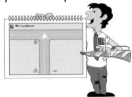

If you cannot find these materials in your local book shop you or your instructor can purchase them direct by contacting Teaching Driving Limited on 01977 600458.

How the LD theory test training programme works

The appropriate theory test lesson would normaly be undertaken before the corresponding practical lesson. Therefore before undertaking driving lesson 1 "Getting moving" you would undertake lesson 1 of the theory test programme i.e. "Pre-driving requirements". Each theory lesson is made up of a Lesson Introduction, a Lesson Study References section and a Lesson Quiz. The answers to each lesson quiz can be found in the "Lesson quiz answers" section of this book.

Each theory lesson can be undertaken in one of two ways. Either you can start each lesson by reading the appropriate sections of the Highway Code (and optionally the other books) as shown by the Lesson Study References or you can start by undertaking the Lesson Quiz. It would be more usual for you to start by undertaking the Lesson Quiz first as most people already have a lot of knowledge on the subject and really only want to find out what they need to learn at this stage. Any questions that were answered incorrectly or that you

were unsure about need to be followed up by studying the appropriate sections of the Highway Code etc as directed by the Lesson Study References.

Apart from the first and last lesson quiz each lesson quiz is made up of 70 questions. The first lesson quiz contains 90 questions and the last contains 88 questions. The official DSA data bank question reference number can be found in brackets after each question number

Once you had completed the full programme of theory test lessons you would move onto the two mock tests at the back of this book.

Finally, just a few days before you take the theory test you should go through all the lesson quizzes again noting any questions you are still getting wrong or are uncertain about. Then for those questions only write out the correct answers in full on a sheet of paper or highlight the correct answers using an highlighter pen. Then go through this list again just before the test. By doing this you will significantly improve your chances of recalling the correct answers.

Lesson Introduction

Each Lesson Introduction will explain the basic contents of the theory lesson, what the lesson aims to achieve and how it links with the practical training programme.

Lesson Study References

Most of the information that you need to correctly answer the Lesson Quiz questions can be found in the Highway Code. Consequently, we have listed the appropriate Highway Code rule or rules, sections, pages etc that apply to each particular theory test question. Rule numbers in blue (e.g. R 122) relate to the new Highway Code due for release in early 1999.

We have also given optional study references to The Driving Manual and Know Your Traffic Signs. In some instances these are the only publications that contain information on the specific question topic. Naturally, if you undertake your theory study while undertaking driving lessons with a professional driving instructor, as recommended in this book, you will also be able to ask your driving instructor for further help and advice.

For simplicity we refer to each of the publications by the following intials:-

HC = Highway Code
DM = The Driving Manual
KYTS = Know Your Traffic Signs

The old Highway Code also has a set of theory notes numbered 1 to 93 at the back under the section "The theory of safe and responsible driving" page 79. If you are required to read one of these notes we will refer to it as "TN" followed by the appropriate number. Similarly, in the Highway Code there is a section on "The road user and the law" page 67. If you are required to refer to one of these items we will prefix the number or letter with the word "LAW".

Please note the references are correct as at publication (i.e. 1st August 1998). Should any of the above books be updated we will be happy to send you a new set of study references for a small fee.

Please contact us on 01977 600458 for details.

Lesson Quiz

To undertake a lesson quiz you will need a sheet of paper to list down your answer or answers to each question. Each question will tell you how many answers to select. Write down the question number followed by the letter or letters (i.e a,b,c,d. etc) pertaining to those answers you think are correct.

If you are the slightest bit unsure of the answer or answers you have given write down a question mark "?" at the end of the line.

Once you have completed all the questions in this manner for any particular theory test lesson please refer to the answers in the "Lesson quiz answers" section of this book to determine which answers are correct and which are not.

If there are any answers that are wrong or any questions that you were unsure about (i.e. as denoted by a "?" question mark) you will need to refer back to the Lesson Study References and read the relevant information in the stated publications for those quiz questions. Following this study if you are still unclear about the right answers please consult an experienced driver or better still your professional driving instructor.

Mock Tests

To help ensure you are fully prepared for the theory test we have included a couple of mock tests at the end of the workbook. Each test contains a properly balanced set of questions as in the real exam. Each of these questions will have been covered earlier as part of the theory test lesson programme. To pass you need to correctly answer 30 out of the 35 questions. If you wish to know more about the theory test itself please refer to the next section.

THEORY TEST FOR DRIVERS
PRACTICE QUESTIONS

Surname

First Names

Booking Ref.

Pro. Licence No.

Centre No.   ENGLISH M.V.

	D	D	M	M	Y	Y	Y	Y
Date								

	H	H	M	M
Time				

GENERAL INSTRUCTIONS
1. For each question you must find the right answer(s) and mark an X in the box next to it.
2. Do not write any comments on your test paper.
3. Two examples have been done to show you how to mark your answers.
4. If you make a mistake cross out your original choice completely

and mark your other choice as shown.

EXAMPLES

E1 — What MUST you have before you are allowed to drive in the UK?

Mark one answer

a ☒ A medical certificate
b ☒ A signed passport photograph
c ☒ A signed driving licence
d ☒ A copy of your birth certificate

E2 — Which TWO would help you to have a safe long journey?

Mark two answers

a ☒ Drive through the town centres
b ☒ Use a map to plan your journey
c ☒ Start out in plenty of time
d ☒ Set a time limit for your journey
e ☒ Avoid having breaks until near the end

P1 — This sign means

Mark one answer

a ☒ follow the tracks
b ☒ slippery road ahead
c ☒ change lanes
d ☒ vehicles liable to pass

P2 — You MUST stop when signalled to do so by which THREE of these?

Mark three answers

a ☒ A police officer
b ☒ A pedestrian
c ☒ A school crossing patrol
d ☒ A bus driver
e ☒ A red traffic light

P3 — What should you use the hard shoulder of a motorway for?

Mark one answer

a ☒ Stopping in an emergency
b ☒ Overtaking
c ☒ Stopping when you are tired
d ☒ Joining the motorway

P4 — What should the driver of the red car do?

Mark one answer

a ☒ Pull out quickly
b ☒ Continue to wait for a safe gap in the traffic
c ☒ Continue to wait until the traffic lights change
d ☒ Gesture to the driver of the white car to ask her to stop

1

Do not go on to the main test until you are told to do so.

Overview

The Driving Standards Agency theory test for cars consists of 35 multiple choice questions.

Associated with each question is a list of potential answers. You need to select the correct answer, or indeed answers (if you are required to select more than one).

You will be given 40 minutes to answer the 35 questions. To pass the test you need to correctly answer 30 out of the 35 questions shown (i.e. 86%).

The examination paper

The test examination paper provided will be in the form of an eight page A4 booklet. See picture opposite. The front page contains space for your personal details and a set of instructions on how to complete the questions and correct mistakes. The front page will also contain some practice questions for you to complete before the test starts.

For each question you need to select the correct answer or answers by placing an 'X' in the box next to the answer or answers (as appropriate) that you think are correct.

Each question will tell you how many answers to select. If you make a mistake and put an 'X' in the wrong box you can cross out that box and place an 'X' in the correct box.

Booking the test

You can obtain a theory test application form from your driving instructor or any driving or theory test centre or by telephoning the theory test enquiry line 0870 0101 372. If you are able to pay by credit or debit card you can book a theory test appointment direct on the same number without the need to complete an application form. You will however, need to quote your driver number from your provisional driving licence.

You can also write direct to the Driving Standards Agency to obtain an application form or apply for the theory test. The address is as follows:-

Driving Standards Agency
P O Box 444
Coventry
CV1 2ZY

Special requirements

Special tests can be arranged for candidates with special needs. For example, people with reading difficulties, dyslexia or physical disabilities. In certain of these instances extra time is allowed to complete the test.

The test can also be provided in several other languages including Welsh, Punjabi, Bengali, Urdu, Hindi, Gujerati and Chinese.

If you can speak English but can not read in the languages provided a member of staff will be available to read through the test on a one-to-one basis. If you cannot read or write in any of the languages provided you are allowed to bring a translator with you. You can only bring a translator who's approved as independent.

These requirements must be made known when booking the test.

What you need to do on the day of the test

On arrival at the theory test centre, candidates must present their appointment card or booking number together with a signed valid Great Britain or Northern Ireland provisional driving licence at the registration desk.

You will also be required to show some form of acceptable photographic evidence to prove you are the person named on the provisional driving licence. For example, a photograph with an appropriately worded declaration on the back signed by a professional driving instructor would suffice. You will also be required to leave any bags, coats or written material at the back of the examination room.

An invigilator will supervise up to 30 candidates at a time under normal exam conditions. Pens will be provided and a clock on the wall will be used to determine when the 40 minutes is complete. You will be notified by post, within about a week, of whether you have passed or failed the exam. Same day results are also available at some centres.

Lesson Introduction

The aim of this lesson is to make you familiar with all the documentation associated with owning a motor car, some basic car maintenance issues and other matters you need to consider before you set off. This lesson would normally be undertaken before you started your driving lessons.

Lesson Study References

Lesson Study References

Lesson Quiz

Question 1 (5.65)
You have been convicted of driving whilst unfit through drink or drugs. You will find this is likely to cause the cost of one of the following to rise considerably. Which one ?

Mark one answer
a) Road fund licence.
b) Insurance premiums.
c) Vehicle test certificate.
d) Driving licence.

Question 2 (12.11)
For which TWO of these must you show your motor insurance certificate?

Mark two answers
a) When a police officer asks you for them
b) When you are taking your driving test
c) When you are taxing your vehicle
d) When buying or selling a vehicle
e) When having an MOT inspection

Question 3 (12.17)
What is the legal minimum insurance cover you must have to drive on public roads?

Mark one answer
a) Personal injury cover
b) Fully comprehensive
c) Third party only
d) Third party, fire and theft

Question 4 (12.16)
Before driving anyone else's motor vehicle you should make sure that

Mark one answer
a) your own vehicle has insurance cover
b) the vehicle owner has third party insurance cover
c) the vehicle is insured for your use
d) the owner has left the insurance documents in the vehicle

Question 5 (12.18)
Your car has third party insurance. What does this cover?

Mark three answers
a) Damage to your own car.
b) Damage to your car by fire.
c) Injury to another person.
d) Damage to someone else's property.
e) Damage to other vehicles.
f) Injury to yourself.

Question 6 (12.19)
The cost of your insurance will be reduced if

Mark one answer
a) your car is large and powerful
b) you are using the car for work purposes
c) you have penalty points on your licence
d) you are over 25 years old.

Question 7 (12.14)
A police officer asks to see your driving documents. You don't have them with you. You may produce them at a police station within

Mark one answer
a) seven days
b) five days
c) 14 days
d) 21 days

Question 8 (12.26)
Which THREE of the following do you need before you can drive legally?

Mark three answers
a) A valid tax disc displayed on your vehicle
b) A current MOT certificate if the car is over three years old
c) A vehicle handbook
d) A valid signed driving licence
e) Proof of your identity
f) Fully comprehensive insurance

Question 9 (13.52)
The police may ask you to produce which three of these documents following an accident?.

Mark three answers
a) Vehicle registration document.
b) Driving licence.
c) Theory test certificate.
d) Insurance certificate.
e) M.o.T. test certificate.
f) Road tax disc.

Question 10 (12.30)
Which THREE pieces of information are found on a vehicle registration document?

Mark three answers
a) Type of insurance cover
b) Make of vehicle
c) Engine size
d) Service history details
e) Date of MOT
f) Registered keeper

Question 11 (12.31)
You have a duty to contact the licensing authority when

Mark three answers
a) you go abroad on holiday
b) you change your vehicle
c) you change your name
d) your job status is changed
e) your permanent address changes
f) your job involves travelling abroad

Question 12 (12.32)
You must notify the licensing authority when

Mark three answers
a) your health affects your driving
b) your eyesight does not meet a set standard
c) you intend lending your vehicle
d) your vehicle requires an MOT certificate
e) you change your vehicle

Question 13 (12.12)
Vehicle excise duty is often called 'Road tax or 'The Tax disc. You must

Mark one answer
a) keep it with your registration document
b) display it clearly on your vehicle
c) keep it concealed safely in your vehicle
d) carry it on you at all times

Question 14 (12.22)
Your car needs an MOT certificate. If you drive without one this could invalidate your

Mark one answer
a) vehicle service record
b) insurance
c) road tax disc
d) vehicle registration document

Question 15 (12.20)
Motorcars and motorcycles must FIRST have a MOT test certificate when they are

Mark one answer
a) Three years old
b) One year old
c) Five years old
d) Seven years old

Question 16 (12.23)
When is it legal to drive a car over three years old without an MOT certificate?

Mark one answer
a) Up to seven days after the old certificate has run out
b) When driving to an appointment at an MOT centre
c) When driving to an MOT centre to make an appointment
d) Just after buying a second-hand car with no MOT

Question 17 (12.24)
Your vehicle needs a current MOT certificate. You do not have one. Until you do have one you will not be able to renew your

Mark one answer
a) driving licence
b) vehicle insurance
c) road tax disc
d) vehicle registration document.

Question 18 (12.21)
An MOT certificate is normally valid for

Mark one answer
a) three years after the date it was issued
b) 10,000 miles.
c) one year after the date it was issued
d) 30,000 miles.

Question 19 (12.25)
Which of these vehicles is not required to have an MOT certificate?

Mark two answers
a) Police vehicle.
b) Small trailer.
c) Ambulance.
d) Caravan.

Question 20 (12.33)
You have just bought a second hand vehicle. When should you tell the licensing authority of change of ownership ?

Mark one answer
a) Immediately.
b) After 28 days.
c) When an MOT is due.
d) Only when you insure it.

Question 21 (12.2)
Your driving licence must be signed by

Mark one answer
a) a police officer
b) a driving instructor
c) your next of kin
d) you

Question 22 (12.1)
To drive on the road learners MUST

Mark one answer
a) apply for a driving test within 12 months
b) have NO penalty points on their licence
c) have a signed, valid provisional licence
d) have taken professional instruction

Question 23 (5.49)
As a provisional licence holder, you must not drive a motor car

Mark two answers
a) at more than 50 mph
b) on your own
c) on the motorway
d) under the age of 18 years of age at night
e) with passengers in the rear seats

Question 24 (9.2)
As a provisional licence-holder you should not drive a car

Mark one answer
a) over 50 mph
b) at night
c) on the motorway
d) with passengers in rear seats.

Question 25 (9.3)
Which FOUR of these must NOT use motorways?

Mark four answers
a) Learner car drivers
b) Double Decker buses
c) Farm tractors
d) Motorcycles over 50cc
e) Horse riders
f) Cyclists

Question 26 (5.66)
What advice should you give to a driver who has had a few alcoholic drinks at a party?

Mark one answer
a) Wait a short while and then drive home.
b) Have a strong cup of coffee and then drive home.
c) Go home by public transport.
d) Drive home carefully and slowly.

Question 27 (5.67)
A driver attends a social event. What precaution should the driver take?

Mark one answer
a) Avoid busy roads after drinking alcohol
b) Drink plenty of coffee after drinking alcohol
c) Avoid drinking alcohol on an empty stomach
d) Avoid drinking alcohol completely

Question 28 (5.56)
Which THREE result from drinking alcohol and driving?

Mark three answers
a) Greater awareness of danger
b) Faster reactions
c) False sense of confidence
d) Poor judgement of speed
e) Less control

Question 29 (5.57)
Which THREE of these are likely effects of drinking alcohol on driving?

Mark three answers
a) Poor judgement
b) Reduced co-ordination
c) Increased concentration
d) Faster reactions
e) Colour blindness
f) Increased confidence

Question 30 (5.63)
How does alcohol affect your driving?

Mark one answer
a) It improves your co-ordination
b) It reduces your concentration
c) It increases your awareness
d) It speeds up your reactions

Question 31 (5.64)
After drinking alcohol heavily you should not drive the following day. Why is this?

Mark two answers
a) You may still be over the legal limit.
b) Your concentration will not be badly affected.
c) You will be well under the legal limit.
d) Your concentration may still be badly affected.

Question 32 (5.68)
It is 8 hours since you last had an alcoholic drink. Which of the following applies?

Mark two answers
a) You will certainly be under the legal limit.
b) You will have no alcohol in your system.
c) You may still be unfit to drive.
d) You may still be over the legal limit.

Question 33 (5.60)
Drinking any amount of alcohol is likely to

Mark three answers
a) reduce your ability to react to hazards
b) increase the speed of your reactions
c) worsen your judgement of speed
d) increase your awareness of danger
e) give a false sense of confidence

Question 34 (5.59)
What is the maximum fine when causing death by careless driving whilst under the influence of alcohol?

Mark one answer
a) A fine of £500
b) An unlimited fine
c) A fine of £2000
d) A fine of £5000

Question 35 (5.61)
You are invited to a pub lunch. You know that you will have to drive in the evening. What is your best course of action?.

Mark one answer
a) avoid mixing your alcoholic drinks.
b) not drink any alcohol at all.
c) have some milk before drinking alcohol.
d) eat a hot meal with your alcoholic drinks.

Question 36 (5.78)
You are taking drugs which are likely to affect your driving. What should you do?

Mark one answer
a) Drive only for short distances
b) Limit your driving to essential journeys
c) Seek medical advice before driving
d) Only drive if accompanied by a full licence holder

Question 37 (5.71)
You are about to return home from holiday when you become ill. A doctor prescribes drugs which are likely to affect your driving.
You should

Mark one answer
a) drive only if someone is with you
b) avoid driving on motorways
c) not drive yourself
d) never drive at more than 30 mph

Question 38 (3.9)
Which THREE does the law require you to keep in good condition?

Mark three answers
a) Gears.
b) Clutch.
c) Headlights.
d) Windscreen.
e) Seat belts.

Question 39 (3.6)
Which FOUR of these must be in good working order for your car to be roadworthy?

Mark four answers
a) Windscreen wipers
b) Speedometer
c) Windscreen washers
d) Oil warning light
e) Horn
f) Temperature gauge

Question 40 (3.10)
New petrol-engined cars must be fitted with catalytic converters. The reason for this is to

Mark one answer
a) control exhaust noise levels
b) prolong the life of the exhaust system
c) allow the exhaust system to be recycled
d) reduce harmful exhaust emissions.

Question 41 (3.64)
You are testing your suspension. You notice that your vehicle keeps bouncing when you press down on the front wing. What does this mean?

Mark one answer
a) Worn tyres.
b) Tyres under-inflated.
c) Steering wheel not located centrally.
d) Worn shock absorbers.

Question 42 (3.18)
Why should tyres be kept to the pressure the manufacturer tells you?

Mark one answer
a) To keep the car the right height off the road.
b) To save wear on the engine.
c) To stop the car from sloping to one side.
d) To help prevent the car from skidding.

Question 43 (3.16)
It is important that tyre pressures are correct. They should be checked at least

Mark one answer
a) once a week
b) every time the vehicle is serviced
c) every four weeks
d) every time the vehicle has an MOT test.

Question 44 (3.19)
Driving with under-inflated tyres can affect

Mark two answers
a) engine temperature
b) fuel consumption
c) braking
d) oil pressure.

Question 45 (3.15)
It is essential that tyre pressures are checked regularly. When should this be done?

Mark one answer
a) After any lengthy journey
b) After driving at high speed
c) When tyres are hot
d) When tyres are cold

Question 46 (3.27)
Excessive or uneven tyre wear can be caused by faults in the

Mark two answers
a) braking system
b) suspension
c) gearbox
d) exhaust system

Question 47 (3.55)
Excessive or uneven tyre wear can be caused by faults in which THREE ?

Mark three answers
a) Wheel alignment
b) The gearbox
c) The exhaust system
d) The accelerator
e) The braking system
f) The suspension

Question 48 (3.25)
The legal minimum depth of tread for car tyres over three-quarters of the breadth is

Mark one answer
a) 1 mm
b) 1.6 mm
c) 4 mm
d) 2.5 mm

Question 49 (3.24)
It is illegal to drive with tyres that

Mark one answer
a) have a large deep cut in the side wall
b) have been bought second-hand
c) are of different makes
d) have painted walls.

Question 50 (3.12)
What can cause heavy steering?

Mark one answer
a) Driving on ice.
b) Badly worn brakes.
c) Over-inflated tyres.
d) Under-inflated tyres.

Question 51 (3.21)
A policeman orders your car to stop.
He finds you have a faulty tyre.
Who is responsible ?

Mark one answer
a) You, the driver.
b) Whoever services the car.
c) The previous owner.
d) Whoever issued the current M.O.T.

Question 52 (14.4)
When travelling for long periods at high speed you should normally

Mark one answer
a) lessen your tyre pressures
b) keep at your regular tyre pressure
c) increase your tyre pressure before leaving
d) increase tyre pressures on your return

Question 53 (14.3)
On whitch TWO occasions should you inflate your tyres to more than the recommended normal pressure?

Mark two answers
a) When the roads are slippery
b) When driving fast for a long distance
c) When the tyre tread is warn below 2mm
d) When carrying a heavy load
e) When the weather is cold
f) When the vehicle is fitted with anti-lock brakes

Question 54 (3.5)
Which of these, if allowed to get low, could cause an accident?

Mark one answer
a) Anti-freeze level
b) Battery water level
c) Radiator coolant level
d) Brake fluid level

Question 55 (3.30)
Your vehicle pulls to one side when braking. You should

Mark one answer
a) use your handbrake at the same time
b) consult your garage as soon as possible
c) pump the pedal when braking
d) change the tyres around

Question 56 (3.4)
Your vehicle pulls to one side when you brake. What is the most likely fault?

Mark one answer
a) Low brake fluid level.
b) Your handbrake is still on
c) Poorly adjusted brakes
d) Incorrect tyre pressures

Question 57 (3.39)
When are you allowed to drive if your brake lights do NOT work?

Mark one answer
a) During the daytime
b) When going for an MOT test
c) In an emergency
d) At no time

Question 58 (3.41)
When may you use hazard warning lights?

Mark one answer
a) When you have broken down
b) To park on double yellow lines
c) To park alongside another car
d) When you are being towed

Question 59 (3.42)
Hazard warning lights should be used when vehicles are

Mark one answer
a) faulty and moving slowly
b) being towed along a road
c) broken down and causing an obstruction
d) reversing into a side road

Question 60 (3.34)
If you notice a strong smell of petrol as you drive along you should

Mark one answer
a) stop and investigate the problem
b) expect it to stop in a few miles
c) not worry, as it is only exhaust fumes
d) carry on at a reduced speed

Question 61 (3.65)
In which of these containers may you carry petrol in a motor vehicle?

 A   B

 C   D

Mark one Answer
a) Container A
b) Container B
c) Container C
d) Container D

Question 62 (13.66)
What TWO safeguards could you take against fire risk to your vehicle?

Mark two answers
a) Keep water levels above maximum.
b) Carry a fire extinguisher.
c) Avoid driving with a full tank of petrol.
d) Use unleaded petrol.
e) Check out any strong smell of petrol.
f) Use low octane fuel.

Question 63 (14.9)
Which THREE are suitable restraints for a child under three years?

Mark three answers
a) An adult holding a child
b) A lap belt
c) An adult seat belt
d) A child seat
e) A baby carrier
f) A harness

Question 64 (14.10)
Your car is fitted with child safety door locks. When used this means that normally

Mark one answer
a) the rear doors can only be opened from the outside
b) the rear doors can only be opened from the inside
c) all the doors can only be opened f from the outside
d) all the doors can only be opened from the inside.

Question 65 (14.12)
Your vehicle is fitted with child safety door locks. You should use these so that children inside the car cannot open.

Mark one answer
a) the right-hand doors
b) the left-hand doors
c) the rear doors
d) any of the doors.

Question 66 (14.11)
What do child locks in a vehicle do?

Mark one answer
a) Lock the rear windows in the up position
b) Stop children from opening rear doors
c) Lock the seat belt buckles in place
d) Stop the rear seats from tipping forward

Question 67 (14.6)
Any load that is carried on a roof rack MUST be

Mark one answer
a) carried only when strictly necessary
b) securely fastened when driving
c) covered with plastic sheeting
d) as light as possible

Question 68 (14.7)
When your vehicle is loaded you MUST make sure that the load will

Mark one answer
a) remain secure
b) be easy to unload
c) not be damaged
d) not damage the vehicle.

Question 69 (14.1)
Overloading your vehicle can seriously affect the

Mark two answers
a) gearbox
b) steering
c) handling
d) battery life
e) journey time

Question 70 (14.8)
You have a heavy load on your roof rack. What effect will it have when you are driving ?

Mark one answer
a) Make the fuel consumption less.
b) Reduce the stopping distance.
c) Make the steering lighter.
d) Reduce stability.

Question 71 (1.7)
Objects hanging from your interior mirror may

Mark two answers
a) Restrict your view
b) Improve your driving
c) Distract your attention
d) Help your concentration

Question 72 (5.88)
Which two things would help to keep you alert during a long motorway journey?

Mark two answers
a) Finishing your journey as fast as you can.
b) Keeping off the motorway and using country roads.
c) Making sure that you get plenty of fresh air.
d) Making regular stops for refreshments.

Question 73 (5.97)
An older persons driving ability could be affected because they may be unable to

Mark one answer
a) understand road signs
b) obtain car insurance
c) react very quickly
d) give signals correctly

Question 74 (9.7)
Why is it particularly important to carry out a check on your vehicle before making a long motorway journey?

Mark one answer
a) The road surface will wear down the tyres faster
b) You will have to do more harsh braking on motorways
c) Motorway service stations do not deal with breakdowns
d) Continuous high speeds may increase the risk of your vehicle breaking down

Question 75 (3.2)
What should you use to check the engine oil level?

Mark one answer
a) Con-rod.
b) Dail gauge.
c) Dipstick
d) Timing light.

Question 76 (3.3)
When must you especially check the engine oil level?

Mark one answer
a) Before a long journey.
b) When the engine is hot.
c) Early in the morning.
d) Every 6000 miles.

Question 77 (3.13)
Your car is fitted with power assisted steering. This will make the steering seem

Mark one answer
a) lighter
b) heavier
c) quieter
d) noisier.

Question 78 (3.28)
There is a vibration on your steering wheel as you drive. You should check that the

Mark one answer
a) doors are closed
b) wheels are balanced
c) exhaust is not loose
d) engine oil level is correct.

Question 79 (3.29)
New tyres should be run in at reasonable speeds for the first

Mark one answer
a) 500 miles
b) 100 miles
c) 10 miles
d) 1000 miles.

Question 80 (3.32)
Your anti-lock brakes warning light stays on. You should

Mark one answer
a) Check the brake fluid level
b) check the footbrake freeplay
c) check that the handbrake is released
d) have the brakes checked immediately.

Question 81 (3.80)
The pictured vehicle is 'environmentally friendly' because it

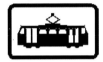

Mark three answers
a) reduces noise pollution
b) uses diesel fuel
c) uses electricity
d) uses unleaded fuel
e) reduces parking spaces
f) reduces town traffic.

Question 82 (3.81)
Driving at 70 mph uses more fuel than driving at 50 mph by up to

Mark one answer
a) 30%
b) 100%
c) 10%
d) 75%.

Question 83 (3.83)
On your vehicle, where would you find a catalytic converter?

Mark one answer
a) In the fuel tank.
b) In the air filter.
c) On the cooling system.
d) On the exhaust system.

21

Question 84 (2.64)
Which of the following are at greatest
risk from other road users?

Mark one answer
a)   Motorcyclists.
b)   Lorry drivers.
c)   Learner car drivers.
d)   Busy bus drivers.

Question 85 (3.11)
Which TWO are badly affected if the
tyres are under-inflated?

Mark one answer
a)   Braking.
b)   Steering.
c)   Changing gear.
d)   Parking.

Question 86 (4.59)
Your indicators may be difficult to see
in bright sunlight. What should you do?

Mark one answer
a)   Put your indicator on earlier.
b)   Give an arm signal as well as
       using your indicator.
c)   Touch the brake several times to
       show the stop lamp.
d)   Turn as quickly as you can.

Question 87 (6.78)
Motorcyclists are particulary vulnerable

Mark one answer
a)   when moving off
b)   on dual carriageways
c)   when approaching junctions
d)   on motorways

Question 88 (14.2)
Who is responsible for making sure
that a vehicle is not overloaded?

Mark one answer
a)   The driver or rider of the vehicle.
b)   The owner of the items being
       carried.
c)   The person who loaded the
       vehicle.
d)   The owner of the vehicle.

Question 89 (5.58)
You find that you need glasses to read
vehicle number plates. When must you
wear them?

Mark one answer
a)   Only when you think it necessary.
b)   At all times when driving.
c)   Only in bad light or at night time.
d)   Only in bad weather conditions.

Question 90 (11.156)
What is the maximum speed on a
single carriageway road?

Mark one answer
a)   50 mph.
b)   60 mph.
c)   40 mph.
d)   70 mph.

Lesson Introduction

The aim of this lesson is to cover the general issues associated with moving away, stopping and parking the car. It covers the basic safety precautions you should make before driving away, some of the procedures associated with moving off and stopping; and where you can and cannot stop or park.

This lesson can be undertaken before you start your driving lessons or after the first driving lesson in the LD practical programme (i.e. lesson 1 "Getting Started").

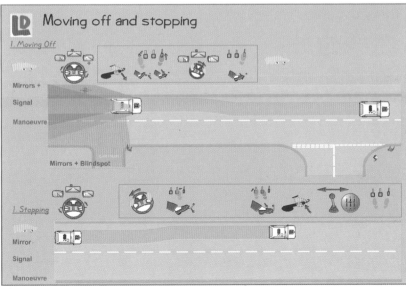

Lesson Study References

Lesson Quiz

Question 1 (8.66)
You are parking on a two way road at night. The speed limit is 40mph. You should park on the

Mark one answer
a) left with sidelights on
b) left with no lights on
c) right with sidelights on
d) right with dipped headlights on

Question 2 (5.51)
A driver can only read a number plate at the required distance with glasses on. The glasses should be worn

Mark one answer
a) all the time when driving
b) only when driving long distances
c) only when reversing
d) only in poor visibility

Question 3 (5.52)
You are about to drive home. You cannot find the glasses you need to wear when driving. You should

Mark one answer
a) borrow a friend's glasses and drive home
b) find a way of getting home without driving
c) drive home at night, so that the lights will help you
d) drive home slowly, keeping to quiet roads

Question 4 (5.50)
To drive you must be able to read a number plate from what distance?

Mark one answer
a) 20.5 metres (67 feet).
b) 10 metres (33 feet).
c) 205 metres (673 feet).
d) 15 meters (49 feet).

Question 5 (5.53)
You must wear glasses or contact lenses when driving on public roads if

Mark one answer
a) you are the holder of an orange badge
b) you cannot read a vehicle number plate from a distance of 36 metres (120 feet without them
c) there is an eyesight problem in your family
d) you cannot read a vehicle number plate from a distance of 20.5 metres (67 feet) without them

Question 6 (5.54)
As a driver you find that your eyesight has become very poor. Your optician says he cannot help you. The law says that you should tell

Mark one answer
a) the licensing authority
b) your own doctor
c) the local police station
d) another optician

Question 7 (5.96)
Just before driving you have had an argument with a member of your family. This has made you angry and late for an appointment. You should

Mark one answer
a) drive as quickly as possible to make up time
b) drive normally, thinking how to calm things down later
c) take a quick drink to calm you down
d) take time to compose yourself before driving

Question 8 (6.40)
You are parking your vehicle in the street. The car parked in front of you is displaying an orange badge. You should

Mark one answer
a) park close to it to save road space
b) allow room for a wheelchair
c) wait until the orange-badge holder returns
d) park with two wheels on the pavement.

Question 9 (3.43)
It is important to wear suitable shoes when you are driving. Why is this?

Mark one answer
a) To maintain control of the pedals
b) To prevent wear on the pedals
c) To enable you to adjust your seat
d) To enable you to walk for assistance if you break down

Question 10 (5.91)
A correct seating position will enable you to

Mark three answers
a) rest your head against the head restraint
b) comfortably reach the pedals
c) have good visibility through the windows
d) talk to all your passengers
e) have a suitable grip on the steering wheel
f) rest your hand on the gear lever

Question 11 (7.12)
You are towing a caravan. Which is the safest type of rear view mirror to use?

Mark one answer
a) Interior wide-angle-view mirror.
b) Extended-arm side mirrors.
c) Ordinary door mirrors.
d) Ordinary interior mirror.

Question 12 (1.8)
The interior mirror of your car should be adjusted so that you can see

Mark one answer
a) through the rear window especially to the nearside
b) straight through the rear side window
c) the rear window and what is happening on the rear seat
d) through the rear window especially to the offside

Question 13 (3.45)
What will reduce the risk of neck injury resulting from a collision?

Mark one answer
a) A collapsible steering wheel
b) A properly adjusted head restraint
c) Anti-lock brakes
d) An air-sprung seat

Question 14 (3.44)
A properly adjusted head restraint will

Mark one answer
a) make you more comfortable
b) help you to avoid neck injury
c) help you to relax
d) help you to maintain your driving position.

Question 15 (3.68)
Why are mirrors on the outside of vehicles often slightly curved (convex)?

Mark one answer
a) They give a wider field of vision.
b) They totally cover blind spots.
c) They make it easier to judge the speed of following traffic.
d) They make following traffic look bigger.

Question 16 (3.52)
You are carrying two children and their parents in your car. Who is responsible for seeing that the children wear seat belts?

Mark one answer
a) The children
b) The children's parents
c) You
d) The front-seat passenger

Question 17 (3.54)
Car passengers MUST wear a seat belt if one is available, unless they are

Mark one answer
a) sitting in the rear-seat
b) exempt for medical reasons
c) under 1.5 metres (5 feet) in height
d) under 14 years old

Question 18 (3.56)
A car driver MUST ensure that seat belts are worn by

Mark one answer
a) all passengers
b) all front-seat passengers
c) all rear-seat passengers
d) children under 14

Question 19 (3.53)
You are driving a friends children home from school. They are both under 14 years old. Who is responsible for making sure they wear a seat belt?

Mark one answer
a) An adult passenger.
b) The children.
c) You, the driver.
d) Your friend.

Question 20 (13.42)
While driving a warning light on your vehicle's instrument panel comes on. You should

Mark one answer
a) continue if the engine sounds alright
b) hope that it is just a temporary electrical fault
c) deal with the problem when there is more time
d) check out the problem quickly and safely.

Question 21 (3.36)
What does this instrument panel light mean when lit ?

Mark one answer
a) Gear lever in park.
b) Gear lever in neutral.
c) Handbrake on.
d) Handbrake off.

Question 22 (3.38)
While driving, this warning light on your dashboard comes on. It means

Mark one answer
a) a fault in the braking system
b) the engine oil is low
c) a rear light has failed
d) your seat belt is not fastened

Question   23 (3.37)
Which instrument panel warning light would show that headlamps are on full beam ?

Mark one answer

 a)   b)

 c)   d)

Question   24 (1.12)
What, according to The Highway Code, do the letters MSM mean?

Mark one answer
a)   Mirror, signal, manoeuvre.
b)   Manoeuvre, signal, mirror.
c)   Mirror, speed, manoeuvre.
d)   Manoeuvre, speed, mirror.

Question   25 (1.6)
As a driver what does the term 'blind spot' mean?

Mark one answer
a)   An area covered by your right hand mirror
b)   An area not covered by your headlamps
c)   An area covered by your left hand mirror
d)   An area not seen in your mirrors

Question   26 (1.3)
To move off safely from a parked position you should

Mark one answer
a)   use your mirrors and look round for a final check
b)   give a hand signal as well as using your indicators
c)   signal if other drivers will need to slow down
d)   NOT look round if there is a parked vehicle close in front of you

Question   27 (1.5)
You are parked on the left . Before you move off you should

Mark one answer
a)   signal right before looking behind and selecting a gear
b)   check mirrors and look round for a final check
c)   rely only on mirrors when looking behind for other traffic
d)   always wait for oncoming traffic to be out of sight

Question   28 (5.20)
What does the solid white line at the side of the road indicate

Mark one answer
a)   traffic lights ahead
b)   edge of carriageway
c)   footpath on the left
d)   cycle path

Question   29 (11.110)
The white line along the side of the road

Mark one answer
a)   shows the edge of the carriageway
b)   shows the approach to a hazard
c)   means no parking
d)   means no overtaking

Question   30 (4.64)
You are about to go down a steep hill. To control the speed of your vehicle you should

Mark one answer
a)   select a low gear and avoid using the brakes
b)   select a high gear and use the brakes firmly
c)   select a high gear and use the brakes carefully
d)   select a low gear and use the brakes carefully

Question   31 (4.65)
You are on a long, downhill slope. What should you do to help control the speed of your vehicle?

Mark one answer
a)   Put the clutch down
b)   Grip the steering wheel tightly
c)   Select a low gear
d)   Select neutral

Question 32 (4.67)
You wish to park facing downhill. What TWO of the following should you do?

Mark two answers
a) Park close to the bumper of another car.
b) Park with two wheels on the kerb.
c) Turn the steering wheel towards the kerb.
d) Put the handbrake on firmly.
e) Turn the steering wheel away from the kerb.

Question 33 (4.69)
When approaching a right-hand bend you should keep well to the left. Why is this?

Mark one answer
a) To let faster traffic from behind overtake
b) To be positioned safely if the vehicle skids
c) To improve your view of the road
d) To overcome the effect of the road's slope

Question 34 (4.70)
You are coming up to a right-hand bend. You should

Mark one answer
a) keep well to the left as it makes the bend faster
b) keep well to the right to make the bend less sharp
c) keep well to the left for a better view around the bend
d) Keep well to the right to avoid anything in the gutter

Question 35 (4.43)
Coasting the vehicle

Mark one answer
a) reduces the driver's control
b) makes steering easier
c) uses more fuel
d) improves the driver's control

Question 36 (8.7)
You shouldn't drive with your foot on the clutch for longer than necessary because it

Mark one answer
a) reduces your control of the vehicle
b) increases wear on the gearbox
c) increases petrol consumption
d) reduces the grip of the tyres

Question 37 (8.4)
What are TWO main reasons why coasting downhill is wrong?

Mark two answers
a) The vehicle will pick up speed
b) It puts more wear and tear on the tyres
c) Petrol consumption will be higher
d) It damages the engine
e) You have less braking and steering control

Question 38 (8.6)
Why is coasting wrong?

Mark one answer
a) It will make the engine stall
b) The engine will run faster
c) It will cause the car to skid
d) There is no engine braking

Question 39 (8.13)
Why is pressing the clutch down for long periods a bad habit?

Mark one answer
a) It reduces the car's speed when going downhill.
b) It causes the engine to wear out more quickly.
c) It reduces the driver's control of the vehicle.
d) It causes the engine to use more fuel.

Question 40 (8.14)
You should avoid 'coasting' your vehicle because it could

Mark one answer
a) damage the suspension
b) increase tyre wear
c) flatten the battery
d) reduce steering control.

Question 41 (1.14)
What is the safest way to brake?

Mark one answer
a) Brake lightly, then harder as you begin to stop, then ease off just before stopping
b) Brake hard, put your gear lever into neutral and pull your handbrake on just before stopping
c) Brake lightly, push your clutch pedal down and pull your handbrake on just before stopping
d) Put your gear lever into neutral, brake hard, then ease off just before stopping

Question 42 (4.5)
When dealing with a bend you should brake

Mark one answer
a) hard before you enter the bend
b) gently before you enter the bend
c) gently as you enter the bend
d) hard as you enter the bend

Question 43 (4.6)
Braking hard at speed on a sharp bend can make your vehicle

Mark one answer
a) more stable
b) unstable
c) stall
d) corner safely

Question 44 (4.23)
When braking hard in a straight line, the weight of the vehicle will shift onto the

Mark one answer
a) front wheels
b) rear wheels
c) left wheels
d) right wheels

Question 45 (4.66)
How can you use the engine of your vehicle as a brake ?

Mark one answer
a) By changing to a lower gear.
b) By selecting reverse gear.
c) By changing to a higher gear.
d) By selecting neutral gear.

Question 46 (8.9)
You are approaching a bend at speed. You should begin to brake

Mark one answer
a) on the bend
b) after the bend
c) after changing gears
d) before the bend.

Question 47 (6.41)
Are you allowed to block the pavement when parking your vehicle?

Mark one answer
a) No, unless to pick up passengers.
b) Yes, when on a narrow road.
c) No, not at any time.
d) Yes, when you think it is safe to do so.

Question 48 (6.21)
In which three places would parking cause an obstruction to others ?

Mark three answers
a) Near the brow of a hill.
b) In a lay by.
c) Where the kerb is raised.
d) Where the kerb has been lowered for wheelchairs.
e) At or near a bus stop.

Question 49 (10.27)
You want to park and you see this sign. On the days and times shown you should

Mark one answer
a) park in a bay and not pay
b) park on yellow lines and pay
c) park on yellow lines and not pay
d) park in a bay and pay.

Question 50 (10.29)
At which of these places are you sometimes allowed to park your vehicle?

Mark one answer
a) On the zigzag lines of a zebra crossing
b) Where there is a single broken yellow line
c) On the nearside lane of a motorway
d) On a clearway

Question 51 (10.19)
You are leaving your vehicle parked on a road. When may you leave the engine running?

Mark one answer
a) If you will be parked for less than five minutes
b) If the battery is flat
c) If there is a passenger in the vehicle
d) Not on any occasion

Question 52 (10.20)
In which FOUR places must you NOT park or wait?

Mark four answers
a) Opposite a traffic island
b) On a dual carriageway
c) On the brow of a hill
d) On the slope of a hill
e) At a bus stop
f) In front of someone else's drive

Question 53 (10.21)
What is the nearest you may park your vehicle to a junction?

Mark one answer
a) 12 metres (40 feet)
b) 10 metres (33 feel)
c) 15 metres (50 feet)
d) 20 metres (65 feel)

Question 54 (10.23)
In which TWO places must you NOT park?

Mark two answers
a) In a side road
b) In a one-way street
c) At a bus stop
d) Near a school entrance
e) Near a police station

Question 55 (10.24)
In which THREE places must you NEVER park your vehicle?

Mark three answers
a) Near the brow of a hill.
b) At or near a bus stop.
c) Where there is no pavement.
d) Within 10 metres (33 feet) of a junction.
e) On a 40 mph road.

Question 56 (10.30)
What MUST you have to park in a disabled space?

Mark one answer
a) An orange badge
b) An advanced driver certificate
c) A modified vehicle
d) A wheelchair

Question 57 (10.31)
You are looking for somewhere to park your vehicle. The area is full EXCEPT for spaces marked 'disabled use'. You must

Mark one answer
a) use these spaces when elsewhere is full
b) stay with your vehicle when you park there
c) use these spaces, disabled or not
d) not park there unless permitted.

Question 58 (10.34)
You can park on the right-hand side of a road at night

Mark one answer
a) in a one-way street
b) with your sidelights on
c) more than 10 metres (33 feet) from a junction
d) under a lamp-post.

Question 59 (10.33)
You park overnight on a road with a 40 mph speed limit. You should

Mark one answer
a) park facing the traffic
b) park with sidelights on
c) park with dipped headlights on
d) park near a street light.

Question 60 (10.32)
Your vehicle is parked on the road at night. When must you use sidelights?

Mark one answer
a) Where you are near a bus stop
b) Where there are continuous white lines in the middle of the road
c) Where you are facing oncoming traffic
d) Where the speed limit exceeds 30 mph

Question 61 (10.28)
What is the meaning of this sign?

Mark one answer
a) No entry.
b) Waiting restrictions.
c) National speed limit.
d) School crossing patrol.

Question 62 (11.21)
What does this sign mean?

Mark one answer
a) National speed limit applies
b) Waiting restrictions apply
c) Waiting permitted
d) Clearway (no stopping)

Question 63 (11.22)
What does this sign mean?

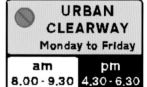

Mark one answer
a) You can park on the days and times shown.
b) No parking on the days and times shown.
c) No parking at all from Monday to Friday.
d) You can park at any time: the urban clearway ends.

Question 64 (11.23)
What does this sign mean?

Mark one answer
a) End of restricted speed area.
b) End of restricted parking area.
c) End of clearway.
d) End of cycle route.

Question 65 (11.27)
What does this sign mean?

Mark one answer
a) Distance to parking place ahead.
b) Distance to public telephone ahead.
c) Distance to public house ahead.
d) Distance to passing place ahead.

Question 66 (10.25)
On a clearway you must not stop

Mark one answer
a) at any time
b) during daylight hours
c) when it is busy
d) in the rush hour

Question 67 (10.26)
You are driving on an urban clearway. You may stop only to

Mark one answer
a) set down and pick up passengers
b) use a mobile telephone
c) ask for directions
d) load or unload goods

Question 68 (11.24)
Which sign means 'no stopping'?

Mark one answer

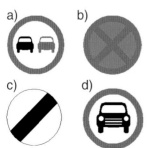

Question 69 (11.25)
What does this sign mean?

Mark one answer
a) Roundabout.
b) Crossroads.
c) No stopping.
d) No entry.

Question 70 (11.26)
You see this sign ahead. It means

Mark one answer
a) No stopping
b) No Entry
c) National speed limit applies
d) Waiting restrictions apply

Lesson Introduction

During this lesson you will become familiar with how to deal with accidents including some very basic first aid. Hopefully you will never have to put this theory into practice. However, even with this limited knowledge you may be able to save a life. You will also start to look at some basic hazards that you may come across and how best to deal with them.

Your ability to deal with an accident is not tested as part of the driving test. This is why this lesson doesn't directly link to the practical training programme. Consequently, we cover it while you are developing basis control skills before driving lesson 3 "Steering".

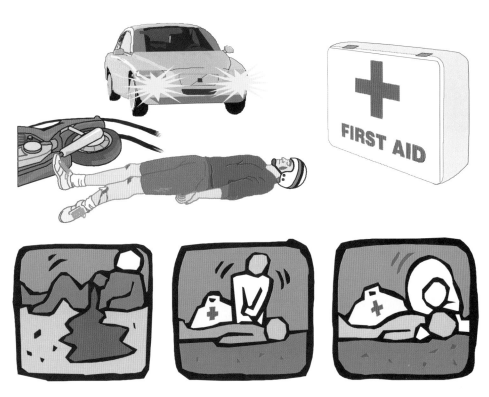

Lesson Study References

Lesson Quiz

Question 1 (2.58)
A person herding sheep asks you to stop. You should

Mark one answer
a) ignore them as they have no authority
b) stop and switch off your engine
c) continue on but drive slowly
d) try and get past quickly

Question 2 (13.8)
You arrive at a serious motorcycle accident. The motorcyclist is unconscious and bleeding. Your main priorities should be to

Mark three answers
a) try to stop the bleeding
b) make a list of witnesses
c) check the casualty's breathing
d) take the numbers of the vehicles involved
e) sweep up any loose debris
f) check the casualty's airways

Question 3 (1.35)
You see an accident on the other side of the road. Your lane is clear. You should

Mark one answer
a) assist the emergency services
b) stop, and cross the road to help
c) concentrate on what is happening ahead
d) place a warning triangle in the road

Question 4 (5.2)
Where would you expect to see these markers?

Mark two answers
a) On a motorway sign.
b) At the entrance to a narrow bridge.
c) On a large goods vehicle.
d) On a builder's skip placed on the road.

Question 5 (5.6)
When approaching a hazard your FIRST reaction should be to

Mark one answer
a) use your footbrake
b) change direction
c) release the accelerator
d) check the mirrors.

Question 6 (5.10)
What should the driver of the red car (arrowed) do?

Mark one answer
a) Sound your horn to tell other drivers where he is
b) Wait until the car blocking the way has moved
c) Squeeze through the gap
d) Wave the driver of the white car to go on

Question 7 (5.16)
You think the driver of the vehicle in front has forgotten to cancel his right indicator. You should

Mark one answer
a) sound your horn before overtaking
b) overtake on the left if there's room
c) flash your lights to alert the driver
d) stay behind and not overtake.

Question 8 (6.84)
An injured motorcyclist is lying unconscious in the road. You should

Mark one answer
a) remove the crash helmet
b) seek medical assistance
c) move the person off the road
d) remove the leather jacket

Question 9 (5.21)
You see this sign ahead. You should expect the road to

Mark one answer
a) go steeply uphill
b) go steeply downhill
c) bend sharply to the left
d) bend sharply to the right

Question 10 (5.35)
While driving, you see this sign ahead. You should

Mark one answer
a) stop at the sign
b) slow, but continue around the bend
c) slow to a crawl and continue
d) stop and look for open farm gates

Question 11 (8.5)
Hills can affect the performance of your vehicle. Which two apply when driving up steep hills ?

Mark two answers
a) Higher gears will pull better.
b) You will slow down sooner.
c) Overtaking will be easier.
d) The engine will work harder.
e) The steering will feel heavier.

Question 12 (9.32)
Which vehicles are normally fitted with amber flashing beacons on the roof?

Mark two answers
a) Doctor's car.
b) Bomb disposal team.
c) Blood transfusion team.
d) Breakdown recovery vehicles.
e) Coastguard.
f) Maintenance vehicles.

Question 13 (8.23)
Motorcyclists are more at risk from other road users because they

Mark one answer
a) are less experienced than other drivers
b) are more likely to brake down than other motorists
c) are always faster than other drivers
d) are more difficult to see than other drivers

Question 14 (10.2)
You may drive on a footpath

Mark one answer
a) to overtake slow-moving traffic
b) when the pavement is very wide
c) if no pedestrians are near
d) to get into a property.

Question 15 (10.72)
At roadworks which of the following can control traffic flow?

Mark three answers
a) A 'stop-go' board.
b) Flashing amber lights.
c) A policeman.
d) Flashing red lights
e) Temporary traffic lights.

Question 16 (11.62)
Which of these signs means there is a series of bends ahead?

Sign a)

Sign b)

Sign c)

Sign d)

Mark one answer
a) Sign A
b) Sign B
c) Sign C
d) Sign D

Question 17 (11.72)
What does this traffic sign mean?

Mark one answer
a) Tyres liable to puncture ahead.
b) Service area ahead.
c) Danger ahead.
d) Slippery road ahead.

Question 18 (11.77)
What does this sign mean?

Mark one answer
a) Quayside or river bank.
b) Steep hill downwards.
c) Slippery road.
d) Road liable to flooding.

Question 19 (11.92)
To avoid an accident when entering a contraflow system, you should

Mark three answers
a) reduce speed in good time
b) switch lanes anytime to make progress
c) chose an appropriate lane early
d) keep the correct separation distance
e) increase speed to pass through quickly
f) follow other motorists closely to avoid long queues

Question 20 (13.7)
You arrive at the scene of a motorcycle accident. The rider is injured. When should the helmet be removed?

Mark one answer
a) Only when it is essential.
b) Always straight away.
c) Only when the motorcyclist asks.
d) Always, unless they are in shock.

Question 21 (13.9)
You arrive at an accident. A motorcyclist is unconscious. Your first priority is the casualty's

Mark one answer
a) breathing
b) bleeding
c) broken bones
d) bruising

Question 22 (11.51)
What are triangular signs for?

Mark one answer
a) To give orders
b) To give directions
c) To give information
d) To give warnings

Question 23 (11.76)
What does this sign mean?

Mark one answer
a) adverse camber.
b) Steep hill downwards.
c) Uneven road
d) Steep hill upwards

Question 24 (13.3)
You are the first to arrive at the scene of an accident. Which FOUR of these should you do?

Mark four answers
a) Move uninjured people away from the vehicles
b) Warn other traffic
c) Call the emergency services
d) Switch off the vehicle engines
e) Leave as soon as another motorist arrives

Question 25 (13.5)
You are the first person to arrive at an accident where people are badly injured. Which THREE should you do?

Mark three answers
a) Move the people who are injured clear of their vehicles.
b) Get people who are not injured clear of the scene.
c) Try and get people who are injured to drink something.
d) Switch on your own hazard warning lights .
e) Make sure someone telephones for an ambulance.

Question 26 (13.16)
You have stopped at the scene of an accident to give help. Which THREE things should you do?

Mark three answers
a) Keep injured people calm by talking to them reassuringly
b) Make sure injured people are not left alone
c) Keep injured people on the move by walking them around
d) Keep injured people warm and comfortable
e) Give injured people a warm drink

Question 27 (13.19)
You arrive at the scene of a motorcycle accident. The rider is conscious but in shock. You should make sure that

Mark one answer
a) the rider is moved to the side of the road
b) the rider is put in the recovery position
c) the rider's helmet is not removed
d) the rider's helmet is removed

Question 28 (13.26)
You arrive at the scene of a motorcycle accident. No other vehicle is involved. The rider is unconcious, lying in the middle of the road. The first thing you should do is

Mark one answer
a) move the rider out of the road
b) warn other traffic
c) clear the road of debris
d) give the rider reassurance.

Question 29 (13.41)
A tanker is involved in an accident. Which sign would show if the tanker is carrying dangerous goods?

Sign A

Sign B

LONG VEHICLE
Sign D

Sign C

Mark one answer
a)   Sign A
b)   Sign B
c)   Sign C
d)   Sign D

Question 30 (13.53)
You are involved in a road accident with another driver. Your vehicle is damaged. Which FOUR of the following should you find out?

Mark four answers
a)   Whether the driver owns the other vehicle involved.
b)   The other drivers name, address and telephone number.
c)   The car make and registration number of the other vehicle.
d)   The occupation of the other driver.
e)   The details of the other drivers vehicle insurance.
f)   Whether the other driver is licenced to drive

Question 31 (13.54)
You have an accident while driving and someone is injured, you do not produce your insurance certificate at the time. You must report it to the police as soon as possible, or in any case within

Mark one answer
a)   24 hours   b)   48 hours
c)   five days   d)   seven days

Question 32 (13.43)
For which TWO should you use hazard warning lights?

Mark two answers
a)   When you slow down quickly on a motorway because of a hazard ahead
b)   When you have broken down
c)   When you need to park on the pavement
d)   When you wish to stop on double yellow lines

Question 33 (13.44)
For which THREE should you use your hazard warning lights?

Mark three answers
a)   When you are temporarily obstructing traffic
b)   When you have broken down
c)   To warn following traffic of a hazard ahead
d)   When you are parking in a restricted area

Question 34 (13.45)
When are you allowed to use hazard warning lights?

Mark one answer
a)   When parked for shopping on double yellow lines
b)   When travelling slowly because you are lost
c)   When stopped and temporarily obstructing traffic
d)   When driving during darkness without headlights

Question 35 (13.46)
When should you switch on your hazard warning lights?

Mark one answer
a)   When you are driving slowly due to bad weather
b)   When you are towing a broken down vehicle
c)   When you cannot avoid causing an obstruction
d)   When you are parked on double yellow lines

Question 36 (13.47)
You have broken down on a two-way road, you have a warning triangle. You should place the warning triangle at least how far from your vehicle?

Mark one answer
a)   25 metres (80 feet)
b)   100 metres (330 feet)
c)   45 metres (149 feet)
d)   5 metres (16 feet)

Question 37 (13.48)
You are in an accident on an (A) class road, you have a warning triangle. At what distance before the obstruction should you place the warning triangle?

Mark one answer
a)   25 metres (80 feet)
b)   100 metres (330 feet)
c)   150 metres (495 feet)
d)   45 metres (149 feet)

Question 38 (13.50)
You break down on an ordinary road, you have a warning triangle. Your warning triangle should be displayed

Mark one answer
a) at least 150 metres (495 feet) behind your vehicle
b) on the roof of your vehicle
c) just behind your vehicle
d) at least 45 metres (149 feet) behind your vehicle

Question 39 (13.51)
Your vehicle is broken down on a straight road. You have a warning triangle. Where should you place it?

Mark one answer
a) Secuely on the roof of your car.
b) 45 metres (47 yards) from your vehicle.
c) 10 metres (11 yards) from your vehicle.
d) Directly ar the rear of your vehicle.

Question 40 (13.4)
An accident has just happened. An injured person is lying in the road. What is the first thing you should do to help?.

Mark one answer
a) Treat the person for shock.
b) Place them in the recovery position.
c) Warn other traffic.
d) Make sure the injured person is kept warm.

Question 41 (13.6)
You are at the scene of an accident and there are several bystanders. Which TWO of the following should you do first?

Mark two answers
a) Always pull people who are hurt out of their vehicles.
b) Ask the bystanders to check the casualties for signs of bleeding.
c) Make sure that the emergency services have been called for.
d) Keep the bystanders clear as they do not know first aid.
e) Clear a parking area for ambulance and fire service crews.

Question 42 (13.10)
An accident has just happened. An injured person is lying in the busy road. What is the first thing you should do to help?

Mark one answer
a) Treat the person for shock.
b) Warn other traffic.
c) Place them in the recovery position.
d) Make sure the injured person is kept warm.

Question 43 (13.2)
At the scene of an accident you must

Mark one answer
a) not put yourself at risk
b) go to those casualties who are screaming
c) pull everybody out of their vehicles
d) leave vehicle engines switched on

Question 44 (13.39)
At an accident it is important to look after the casualty. When the area is safe, you should

Mark one answer
a) get them out of the vehicle
b) give them a drink
c) give them something to eat
d) keep them in the vehicle

Question 45 (13.1)
Which of these items should you carry in your vehicle for use in the event of an accident?

Mark three answers
a) Road map.
b) Bottle of water.
c) Jump leads.
d) Fire extinguisher.
e) First Aid kit.
f) Warning triangle.

Question 46 (13.11)
At an accident a casualty is unconscious. Which three of the following should you check urgently?

Mark three answers
a) Circulation.
b) Airway.
c) Shock.
d) Breathing.
e) Broken bones.

Question 47 (13.13)
You arrive at the scene of an accident. It has just happened and someone is unconscious. Which of the following should be given urgent priority to help them?

Mark three answers
a) Clear the airway and keep it open.
b) Try to get them to drink water.
c) Check that they are breathing.
d) Look for any witnesses.
e) Stop any heavy bleeding.
f) Take the numbers of vehicles involved.

Question 48 (13.15)
At an accident someone is unconscious. Your main priorites should be to

Mark three answers
a) Sweep up tthe broken glass
b) take the names of whitnesses
c) count the number of vehicles involved
d) check the airway is clear
e) make sure they are breathing
f) stop any heavy bleeding

Question 49 (13.37)
At an accident a casualty is unconscious but still breathing. You should only move them if

Mark one answer
a) an ambulance is on its way
b) bystanders advise you to
c) there is further danger
d) bystanders will help you to

Question 50 (13.17)
You arrive at the scene of an accident. It has just happened and someone is injured. Which of the following should be given urgent priority?

Mark three answers
a) Stop any severe bleeding.
b) Get them a warm drink.
c) Check that their breathing is OK.
d) Take numbers of vehicles involved.
e) Look for witnesses.
f) Clear their airway and keep it open.

Question 51 (13.32)
You arrive at an accident where someone is suffering from severe burns. You should

Mark one answer
a) apply lotions to the injury
b) burst any blisters
c) remove anything stuck to the burns
d) douse the burns with cool liquid

Question 52 (13.33)
You arrive at an accident where someone is suffering from severe burns. You should

Mark one answer
a) burst any blisters
b) douse the burns thoroughly with cool liquid
c) apply lotions to the injury
d) remove anything sticking to the burns

Question 53 (13.31)
You arrive at the scene of an accident. There has been an engine fire and someone's hands and arms have been burnt. You should NOT

Mark one answer
a) douse the burn thoroughly with cool liquid
b) lay the casualty down
c) remove anything sticking to the burn
d) remove smouldering clothing

Question 54 (13.21)
Which of the following should you not do at the scene of an accident?

Mark one answer
a) Warn other traffic by switching on your hazard warning lights.
b) Call the emergency services immediatly.
c) Offer someone a cigarette to calm them down.
d) Ask drivers to switch off their engins.

Question 55 (13.38)
At an accident you suspect a casualty has back injuries. The area is safe. You should

Mark one answer
a) offer them a drink
b) not move them
c) raise their legs
d) offer them a cigarette

Question 56 (13.12)
In first aid what does ABC stand for?

Mark three answers
a) Circulation.
b) Alert.
c) Bleeding.
d) Conscious.
e) Airway.
f) Breathing.

Question 57 (13.14)
Which of the following safety checks is in the correct order?

Mark one answer
a) Breathing - Circulation - Airway.
b) Airway - Breathing - Circulation.
c) Circulation - Breathing - Airway.
d) Breathing - Airway - Circulation.

Question 58 (13.27)
At an accident a small child is not breathing. When giving mouth to mouth you should blow

Mark one answer
a) sharply
b) gently
c) heavily
d) rapidly

Question 59 (13.28)
To start mouth to mouth on a casualty you should

Mark three answers
a) tilt the head forward
b) clear the airway
c) turn them on their side
d) tilt their head back
e) pinch the nostrils together
f) put their arms across their chest

Question 60 (13.29)
You are giving mouth to mouth to a casualty. They are still not breathing on their own. You should

Mark one answer
a) give up if you think they are dead
b) only keep trying for up to two minutes
c) carry on until an ambulance arrives
d) only keep trying for up to four minutes

Question 61 (13.30)
When you are giving mouth to mouth you should only stop when

Mark one answer
a) you think the casualty is dead
b) the casualty can breath without help
c) the casualty has turned blue
d) you think the ambulance is coming

Question 62 (13.22)
When treating someone for shock you should

Mark two answers
a) reassure them
b) loosen tight clothes
c) walk them around
d) give them a hot drink
e) offer them an alcoholic drink

Question 63 (13.23)
You are at the scene of an accident. The driver is suffering from shock. You should

Mark two answers
a) give them a drink
b) re-assure them
c) not leave them alone
d) offer them a cigarette
e) ask who caused the accident

Question 64 (13.24)
You are at the scene of an accident. Someone is suffering from shock. You should

Mark three answers
a) offer them a cigarette
b) offer them a warm drink
c) keep them warm
d) loosen any tight clothing
e) re-assure them constantly

Question 65 (13.25)
You have to treat someone for shock at the scene of an accident. You should

Mark one answer
a) re-assure them constantly
b) walk them around to calm them down
c) give them something cold to drink
d) cool them down as soon as possible

Question 66 (13.20)
You are at the scene of an accident, someone is suffering from shock. You should FOUR

Mark ~~three~~ answers
a) re-assure them constantly
b) offfer them a cigarette
c) Keep them warm
d) avoid moving them if possible
e) loosen any tight clothing
f) give them a warm drink

Question 67 (13.18)
At an accident a casualty has stopped breathing. You should

Mark two answers
a) remove anything that is blocking the mouth
b) keep the head tilted forwards as far as possible
c) raise the legs to help with circulation
d) try to give the casualty something to drink
e) keep the head tilted back as far as possible

Question   68 (13.35)
You arrive at the scene of an accident.
A passenger is bleeding badly from an
arm wound What should you do?

Mark one answer
a)   Apply pressure over the wound
     and keep the arm down.
b)   Dab the wound.
c)   Get them a drink.
d)   Apply pressure over the wound
     and raise the arm.

Question   69 (13.36)
You arrive at the scene of an accident.
A pedestrian is bleeding heavily from a
leg wound but the leg is not broken.
What should you do?

Mark one answer
a)   Dab the wound to stop the
     bleeding.
b)   Keep both legs flat on the ground.
c)   Apply firm pressure to the wound.
d)   Fetch them a warm drink.

Question   70 (13.34)
You arrive at the scene of an accident.
A pedestrian has severe bleeding
wound on their leg although it is not
broken. What should you do?

Mark two answers
a)   Dab the wound to stop the
     bleeding.
b)   Keep both legs flat on the ground.
c)   Apply firm pressure to the wound.
d)   Raise the leg to lessen bleeding.
d)   Fetch them a warm drink.

Lesson Introduction

After driving lesson 4 your instructor would begin to introduce the set manoeuvres starting with the straight line reverse. This is why we cover all the theory questions on manoeuvres at this stage. We also cover general road markings and signs not specifically relevant to later driving lessons.

This theory lesson would be undertaken before practical lesson 4 "Co-ordination".

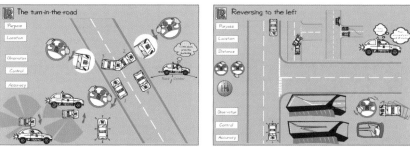

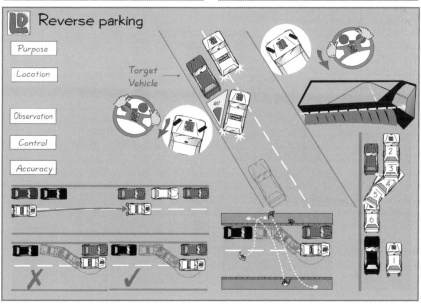

Lesson Study References

Lesson Quiz

Question 1 (1.1)
When turning your car in the road you should

Mark one answer
a) check all around for other road users
b) use a driveway if possible
c) overhang the kerb
d) keep your hand on the handbrake throughout

Question 2 (3.69)
You cannot see clearly behind when reversing. What should you do?

Mark one answer
a) Ask someone to guide you
b) Open your window to look behind
c) Look in the nearside mirror
d) Open the door and look behind

Question 3 (6.12)
You want to reverse into a side road. You are not sure that the area behind your car is clear. What should you do?

Mark one answer
a) Look through the rear window only.
b) Get out and check.
c) Check the mirrors only.
d) Carry on, assuming it's clear.

Question 4 (6.14)
You are reversing from a driveway and cannot see clearly. There are many pedestrians around. You should

Mark one answer
a) continue whilst sounding your horn
b) continue with your hazard lights on
c) get someone to guide you
d) continue: it is your right of way.

Question 5 (6.17)
You are reversing around a corner when you notice a pedestrian walking behind you. What should you do?

Mark one answer
a) Slow down and wave the pedestrian across.
b) Continue reversing and steer round the pedestrian.
c) Stop and give way.
d) Continue reversing and sound your horn.

Question 6 (6.15)
Who is especially in danger of not being seen as you reverse your car ?

Mark one answer
a) Motorcyclist.
b) Car drivers.
c) Cyclist.
d) Children.

Question 7 (6.13)
You are about to reverse into a side road. A pedestrian wishes to cross behind you. You should

Mark one answer
a) wave to the pedestrian to stop
b) wave to the pedestrian to cross
c) reverse before the pedestrian starts to cross
d) give way to the pedestrian

Question 8 (10.82)
You are on a busy main road and find you are travelling in the wrong direction. What should you do?

Mark one answer
a) Make a 'three-point' turn in the main road
b) Turn into a side road on the right and reverse into the main road
c) Turn round in a side road
d) Make a U-turn in the main road

Question 9 (10.86)
You are parked in a busy high street. What is the safest way to turn your vehicle around to go the opposite way?

Mark one answer
a) Find a quiet side road to turn round in
b) Get someone to stop the traffic
c) Do a U-turn
d) Drive into a side road and reverse into the main road

Question 10 (10.85)
You MUST NOT reverse

Mark one answer
a) for longer than necessary
b) for more than a cars length
c) into a side road
d) in a built-up area

Question 11 (10.88)
When may you reverse from a side road into a main road?

Mark one answer
a) NOT at any time
b) Only if both roads are clear of traffic
c) At any time
d) Only if the main road is clear of traffic

Question 12 (10.84)
You may remove your seat belt when carrying out a manoeuvre that involves

Mark one answer
a) reversing
b) a hill start
c) an emergency stop
d) driving slowly.

Question 13 (10.87)
When you're NOT sure that it's safe to reverse your vehicle you should

Mark one answer
a) use your horn.
b) rev your engine.
c) get out and check.
d) reverse slowly.

Question 14 (10.89)
You are reversing your vehicle into a side road. When would the greatest hazard to passing traffic occur?

Mark one answer
a) After you have completed the manoeuvre.
b) Just before you actually begin to manoeuvre.
c) After you have entered the side road.
d) When the front of your vehicle swings out.

Question 15 (5.5)
Which road user has caused a hazard

Mark one answer
a) The moving car
b) The car turning
c) The parked car
d) The pedestrian waiting to cross

Question 16 (5.9)
What THREE things should the driver of the grey (arrowed) car be specially aware of?

Mark three answers
a) Pedestrians stepping out between cars
b) Empty parking spaces
c) Cars leaving parking spaces
d) Parked cars' doors opening
e) Other cars behind the grey car
f) The bumpy road surface

Question 17 (6.20)
In which THREE places would parking your vehicle cause danger or obstruction to other road users?

Mark three answers
a) At or near a bus stop
b) On your driveway
c) In a marked parking space
d) In front of a property entrance
e) On the approach to a level crossing

Question 18 (10.57)
You may make a U-turn

Mark one answer
a) when it is safe on a wide road
b) on a motorway, when it is safe
c) in a wide one-way street
d) by mounting both pavements carefully.

Question 19 (10.83)
You should only make a 'U' turn on a

Mark one answer
a) motorway
b) one way street
c) narrow road
d) wide quiet road

Question 20 (11.79)
What does this sign mean?

Mark one answer
a) Humpback bridge.
b) Traffic calming hump.
c) Low bridge.
d) Uneven road.

Question 21 (11.80)
What does this sign mean?

Mark one answer
a) Turn left for parking area.
b) No through road on the left.
c) No entry for traffic turning left.
d) Turn left for ferry terminal.

Question 22 (11.82)
Which sign means 'no through road'?

Mark one answer

Sign A   Sign B

Sign C   Sign D

Question 23 (11.83)
Which of these signs means no through road ?

Mark one answer

a) b)

c) d)

Question 24 (11.81)
What does this sign mean ?

Mark one answer
a)   T junction.
b)   No through road.
c)   Telephone box ahead.
d)   Toilet ahead.

Question 25 (11.1)
You must obey signs giving orders. These signs are mostly in

Mark one answer
a)   Red circles
b)   Red triangles
c)   Blue triangles
d)   Green rectangles

Question 26 (11.2)
Traffic signs giving orders are generally which shape?

Sign A   **Sign B**

Sign D

Sign C

Mark one answer
a)   Sign A
b)   Sign B
c)   Sign C
d)   Sign D

Question 27 (11.3)
Which type of sign tells you NOT to do something?

Sign A   **Sign B**

Sign C   **Sign D**

Mark one answer
a)   Sign A
b)   Sign C
c)   Sign D
d)   Sign B

Question 28 (11.5)
Which sign means no motor vehicles are allowed?

Sign A   **Sign B**

Sign C   **Sign D**

Mark one answer
a)   Sign A
b)   Sign B
c)   Sign C
d)   Sign D

Question 29 (11.6)
Which sign means NO motor vehicles allowed?

Sign A   **Sign B**

Sign C   **Sign D**

Mark one answer
a)   Sign A
b)   Sign B
c)   Sign C
d)   Sign D

Question 30 (11.9)
What does this sign mean?

Mark one answer
a)   Clearway (no stopping)
b)   Cars and motorcycles only
c)   No motor vehicles
d)   No overtaking

47

Question 31 (11.6)
Which of these signs means no motor vehicles?

Sign A

Sign B

Sign C

Sign D

Mark one answer
a) Sign A
b) Sign B
c) Sign C
d) Sign D

Question 32 (11.10)
What does this sign mean?

Mark one answer
a) No parking.
b) No road markings.
c) No through road.
d) No entry.

Question 33 (11.12)
Which sign means 'no entry'?

Mark one answer

Sign A

Sign B

Sign C

Sign D

Question 34 (11.45)
Which of these signs means that you are entering a one-way street?

Mark one answer

Sign A

Sign B

Sign C

Sign D

Question 35 (11.46)
Where would you see a contraflow bus and cycle lane?

Mark one answer
a) On a dual carriageway.
b) On a roundabout.
c) On an urban motorway.
d) On a one-way street.

Question 36 (2.54)
You are driving in a busy one way street. What sould you be most aware of?

Mark one answer
a) Empty parking spaces.
b) Local bus stops
c) Vehicles overtaking on either side.
d) Pedestrians on the pavement.

Question 37 (5.98)
You enter a one-way street by mistake. you should

Mark one answer
a) reverse out of the road
b) turn round in the school enterance
c) continue to the end of the road
d) reverse into a driveway

Question 38 (11.66)
What does this sign mean?

Mark one answer
a) Two-way traffic ahead.
b) Two-way traffic crossing a one-way street.
c) Two-way traffic over a bridge.
d) Two-way traffic crosses a two-way road.

Question 39 (4.39)
Which sign means 'two-way traffic crosses a one-way road'?

Mark one answer

Sign A

Sign B

Sign C

Sign D

Question 40 (11.42)
What does this sign mean?

Mark one answer
a) Give way to oncoming vehicles.
b) Approaching traffic passes you on both sides.
c) Turn off at the next available junction.
d) Pass either side to get to the same destination.

48

Question 41 (11.44)
What does a circular traffic sign with a blue background do?

Mark one answer
a) Give an instruction
b) Give directions
c) Give warning of a motorway ahead
d) Give motorway information

Question 42 (11.28)
What does this sign mean?

Mark one answer
a) Vehicles may not park on the verge or footway.
b) Vehicles may park on the left-hand side of the road only.
c) Vehicles may park fully on the verge or footway.
d) Vehicles may park on the right-hand side of the road only.

Question 43 (11.84)
What does this sign mean ?

Mark one answer
a) Direction to park and ride car park.
b) No parking for buses or coaches.
c) Directions to bus and coach park.
d) Parking area for cars and coaches.

Question 44 (11.86)
Which is the sign for a ring road?

Mark one answer

Sign A   Sign B

Sign C   Sign D

Question 45 (11.87)
What does this sign mean?

Mark one answer
a) Ring road
b) Route for lorries
c) Roundabout
d) Rest area

Question 46 (11.88)
What does this sign mean?

Mark one answer
a) Railway station
b) Ring road
c) Scenic route
d) Route for cyclist

Question 47 (11.49)
What does a sign with a brown background show?

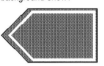

Mark one answer
a) Motorway routes
b) Primary roads
c) Tourist directions
d) Minor routes

Question 48 (11.50)
This sign means

Mark one answer
a) tourist attraction
b) beware of trains
c) level crossing
d) beware of trams

Question 49 (11.89)
What does this sign mean?

Mark one answer
a) Hilly road.
b) Humps in road.
c) Holiday route.
d) Hospital route.

Question 50 (1.32)
Why are these yellow lines painted across the road?

Mark one answer
a) To help you choose the correct lane.
b) To help you keep the correct seperation distance.
c) To make you aware of your speed.
d) To tell you the distance to the roundabout.

Question 51 (8.69)
A rumble device is designed to

Mark two answers
a) give directions
b) prevent cattle escaping
c) alert drivers to low tyre pressure
d) alert drivers to a hazard.
e) encourage drivers to reduce speed.

Question 52 (8.75)
Which of these plates normally appear with this road sign?

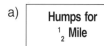

Mark one answer

a)

Humps for
$\frac{1}{2}$ Mile

b)
Hump Bridge

c)
Low Brige

d)
Soft Verge

Question 53 (10.42)
You may drive a motor car in this bus lane

Mark one answer
a) outside its operation hours
b) to get to the front of a traffic queue
c) at no times at all
d) to overtake slow moving traffic.

Question 54 (10.43)
As a car driver which THREE lanes must you NOT use?

Mark three answers
a) Crawler lane
b) Acceleration lane
c) Overtaking lane
d) Bus lane at the times shown
e) Cycle lane
f) Tram lane

Question 55 (10.48)
You are approaching a busy junction. There are several lanes with road markings. At the last moment you realise that you are in the wrong lane. You should

Mark one answer
a) continue in that lane
b) force your way across
c) stop until the area has cleared
d) use clear arm signals to cut across.

Question 56 (11.112)
When may you cross a double solid white line in the middle of the road?

Mark one answer
a) To pass traffic that is queuing back at a junction.
b) To pass a car signalling to turn left ahead.
c) To pass a road maintenance vehicle travelling at 10 mph or less.
d) To pass a vehicle that is towing a trailer.

Question 57 (11.113)
A white line along the centre of a road is a

Mark one answer
a) bus lane marking
b) hazard warning
c) give way marking
d) lane marking

Question 58 (11.118)
Which is a hazard warning line?

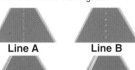

Line A   Line B

Line C   Line D

Mark one answer
a) Line A
b) Line B
c) Line C
d) Line D

Question 59 (11.115)
What does this road marking mean?

Mark one answer
a) No stopping allowed
b) Do not cross the line
c) You are approaching a hazard
d) No overtaking allowed

Question 60 (10.7)
You are driving along a road which has no traffic signs. There are street lights. What is the speed limit?

Mark one answer
a) 60 mph
b) 40 mph
c) 30 mph
d) 20 mph

Question 61 (10.8)
There are no speed limit signs on the road. How is a 30 mph limit indicated?

Mark one answer
a) By street lighting
b) By hazard warning lines
c) By pedestrian islands
d) By double or single yellow lines

Question 62 (10.9)
Where you see street lights but no speed limit signs the limit is usually

Mark one answer
a) 40 mph
b) 30 mph
c) 60 mph
d) 50 mph

Question 63 (10.40)
You are entering an area of roadworks. There is a temporary speed limit displayed. You must

Mark one answer
a) not exceed the speed limit
b) obey the limit only during rush hour
c) accept the speed limit as advisable
d) obey the limit except for overnight.

Question 64 (10.41)
While driving, you approach roadworks. You see a temporary maximum speed limit sign. You must

Mark one answer
a) comply with the sign during the working day
b) comply with the sign at all times
c) comply with the sign when the lanes are narrow
d) comply with the sign during the hours of darkness.

Question 65 (11.4)
What does this sign mean?

Mark one answer
a) Maximum speed limit with traffic calming.
b) Minimum speed limit with traffic calming.
c) '20 cars only' parking zone.
d) Only 20 cars allowed at any one time.

Question 66 (11.7)
What does this sign mean?

Mark one answer
a) New speed limit 20 mph.
b) No vehicles over 30 tonnes.
c) Minimum speed limit 30 mph.
d) End of 20 mph zone.

Question 67 (11.64)
What does this sign mean?

Mark one answer
a) Humpback bridge.
b) Humps in the road.
c) Entrance to tunnel.
d) Steep hill upwards.

Question 68 (11.117)
Where would you see this road marking?

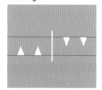

Mark one answer
a) At traffic lights.
b) On road humps.
c) Near a level crossing.
d) At a box junction.

Question 69 (1.2)
Before you make a U-turn, in the road
you shoud

Mark one answer
a) look over your shoulder for a final check
b) signal so that other drivers can slow down for you
c) give arm signals as well as use your indicators
d) select a higher gear than normal

Question 70 (11.93)
You are travelling uphill when you see this sign. Who does it apply to?

Mark one answer
a) Large goods vehicles only.
b) Any slow moving vehicles.
c) Left turning vehicles.
d) Vehicles coming to a halt.

Lesson Introduction

In preparation for the Emergency Stop exercise this lesson covers all the issues associated with emergency situations and speed. It covers all the factors that will effect your stopping distance, how to recognise emergency situations and how to comply with speed restrictions.

This theory lesson would be undertaken before practical lesson 5 "Emergency Stop".

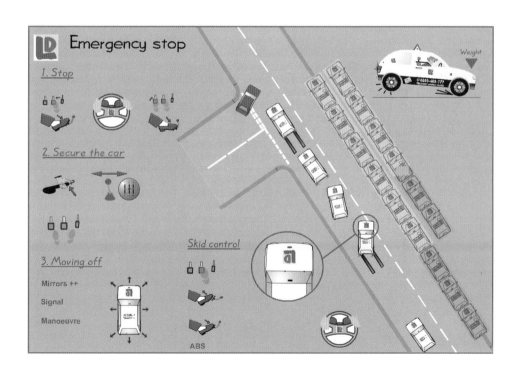

Lesson Study References

Lesson Quiz

Question 1 (1.15)
You are driving on a wet road. You have to stop your vehicle in an emergency. You should

Mark one answer
a) apply the handbrake and footbrake together
b) keep both hands on the wheel
c) select reverse gear
d) give an arm signal.

Question 2 (2.37)
Which THREE of the following emergency vehicles will use blue flashing beacons?

Mark three answers
a) Motorway maintenance.
b) Bomb disposal team.
c) Blood transfusion.
d) Police vehicle.
e) Breakdown recovery vehicle.

Question 3 (2.38)
Which THREE of these emergency services might have blue flashing beacons?

Mark three answers
a) Coastguard.
b) Bomb disposal team.
c) Gritting lorries.
d) Animal ambulances.
e) Mountain rescue.
f) Doctors' cars.

Question 4 (2.41)
What type of emergency vehicle is fitted with a green flashing beacon?

Mark one answer
a) Doctor's car.
b) Road gritter.
c) Ambulance.
d) Fire engine.

Question 5 (2.39)
When being followed by an ambulance showing a flashing blue beacon you should

Mark one answer
a) pull over as soon as safely possible to let it pass
b) accelerate hard to get away from it
c) ignore it if possible, let it pass if forced to
d) brake harshly and immediately stop in the road

Question 6 (2.43)
A vehicle has a flashing green light. What does this mean?

Mark one answer
a) A vehicle is carrying hazardous chemicals.
b) A doctor is answering an emergency call.
c) It is a motorway police patrol vehicle.
d) The vehicle is slow moving.

Question 7 (2.42)
A flashing green beacon on a vehicle means

Mark one answer
a) police on non-urgent duties
b) doctor on an emergency call
c) road safety patrol operating
d) gritting in progress.

Question 8 (2.40)
You see a car showing a flashing green beacon. Should you give way to it ?

Mark one answer
a) Yes, it is a doctor going to an emergency.
b) Yes, it is a fire crew support vehicle.
c) No, it is a slow moving vehicle.
d) No, it is a breakdown vehicle.

Question 9 (6.96)
What is the most common factor in causing road accidents?

Mark one answer
a) Driver error
b) Weather conditions
c) Road conditions
d) Mechanical failure

Question 10 (6.99)
You have just passed your driving test. How likely are you to have an accident compared with other drivers?

Mark one answer
a) More likely
b) About the same
c) It depends on your age
d) Less likely

Question 11 (6.29)
You are driving past parked cars. You notice a wheel of a bicycle sticking out between them. What should you do?

Mark one answer
a) Accelerate past quickly and sound your horn.
b) Slow down and wave the cyclist across.
c) Brake sharply and flash your headlights.
d) Slow down and be prepared to stop for a cyclist.

Question 12 (6.97)
You have a collision whilst your car is moving. What is the FIRST thing you MUST do?

Mark one answer
a) Stop only if there are injured people.
b) Call the emergency services.
c) Stop at the scene of the accident.
d) Call your insurance company.

Question 13 (13.59)
Your tyre bursts while you are driving.
Which TWO should you do?

Mark two answers
a) Select reverse gear to stop the vehicle
b) Give a stopping arm signal and use the gears to slow down
c) Pull up slowly at the side of the road
d) Stop the vehicle by braking as quickly as possible
e) Hold the steering wheel firmly to keep control

Question 14 (13.60)
Which TWO things should you do when a front tyre bursts?

Mark two answers
a) Let the vehicle roll to a stop
b) Brake firmly and quickly
c) Grip the steering wheel firmly
d) Hold the steering wheel lightly
e) Change down and brake hard

Question 15 (4.9)
You are driving at 50mph in good conditions. What would be your shortest stopping distance?

Mark one answer
a) 73 metres (240 feet)
b) 23 metres (75 feet)
c) 53 metres (175 feet)
d) 36 metres (120 feet)

Question 16 (4.10)
You are travelling at 50 mph on a good, dry road. What is your shortest overall stopping distance?

Mark one answer
a) 75 metres (245 feet).
b) 96 metres (315 feet).
c) 53 metres (175 feet).
d) 36 metres (120 feet).

Question 17 (4.8)
What is the shortest stopping distance at 70 mph?

Mark one answer
a) 53 metres (175 feet)
b) 60 metres (200 feet)
c) 73 metres (240 feet)
d) 96 metres (315 feet)

Question 18 (4.16)
Your overall stopping distance will be much longer when driving

Mark one answer
a) in the rain
b) in strong winds
c) in fog
d) at night

Question 19 (4.11)
What is the shortest overall stopping distance on a dry road from 60 mph?

Mark one answer
a) 73 metres (240 feet)
b) 96 metres (315 feet)
c) 53 metres (175 feet)
d) 58 metres (190 feet)

Question 20 (4.2)
You are on a good, dry road surface and in a vehicle with good brakes and tyres. What is the shortest overall stopping distance at 40 mph?

Mark one answer
a) 96 metres (315 feet)
b) 23 metres (75 feet)
c) 53 metres (175 feet)
d) 36 metres (120 feet)

Question 21 (4.20)
What is the main reason why your stopping distance is longer after heavy rain?

Mark one answer
a) You may not be able to see large puddles
b) Your tyres will have less grip on the road
c) The brakes will be cold because they are wet
d) Water on the windscreen will blur your view of the road ahead

Question 22 (4.31)
Freezing conditions will affect the distance it takes you to come to a stop. You should expect stopping distances to increase by up to

Mark one answer
a) two times
b) five times
c) three times
d) ten times

Question 23 (4.1)
Stopping in good conditions at 30 mph takes at least

Mark one answer
a) six car lengths
b) three car lengths
c) two car lengths
d) one car length

Question 24 (8.8)
Which THREE of the following will affect your stopping distance?

Mark three answers
a) The street lighting
b) The time of day
c) The weather
d) How fast you are going
e) The tyres on your vehicle

Question 25 (4.3)
What is the braking distance at 50 mph?

Mark one answer
a)   24 metres (79 feet)
b)   14 metres (45 feet)
c)   55 metres (180 feet)
d)   38 metres (125 feet)

Question 26 (2.29)
You are driving in traffic at the speed limit for the road. The driver behind is trying to overtake. You should

Mark one answer
a)   move closer to the car ahead, so the driver behind has no room to overtake
b)   wave the driver behind to overtake when it is safe
c)   accelerate to get away from the driver behind
d)   keep a steady course and allow the driver behind to overtake

Question 27 (4.32)
When driving in icy conditions, the steering becomes light because the tyres

Mark one answer
a)   have less grip on the road
b)   have more grip on the road
c)   are too hard
d)   are too soft

Question 28 (4.33)
You are driving on an icy road. How can you avoid wheelspin?

Mark one answer
a)   Brake gently and repeatedly
b)   Drive in a low gear at all times
c)   Drive at a slow speed in as high a gear as possible
d)   Use the handbrake if the wheels start to slip

Question 29 (4.36)
How can you avoid wheelspin when driving in freezing conditions?

Mark one answer
a)   Stay in first gear all the time
b)   Put on your handbrake If the wheels begin to slip
c)   Drive in as high a gear as possible
d)   Allow the vehicle to coast in neutral

Question 30 (4.37)
You are driving in freezing conditions. Which TWO should you do when approaching a sharp bend?

Mark two answers
a)   Gently apply your handbrake
b)   Avoid sudden steering movements
c)   Slow down before you reach the bend
d)   Accelerate into the bend
e)   Position towards the middle of the road

Question 31 (4.38)
You are driving in freezing conditions. What should you do when approaching a sharp bend?

Mark two answers
a)   Slow down before you reach the bend.
b)   Gently apply your handbrake.
c)   Firmly use your footbrake.
d)   Coast into the bend.
e)   Avoid sudden steering movements.

Question 32 (4.34)
Skidding is mainly caused by

Mark one answer
a)   the weather
b)   the driver
c)   the vehicle
d)   the road.

Question 33 (4.40)
You are turning left on a slippery road. The back of your vehicle slides to the right. You should

Mark one answer
a)   brake firmly and not turn the steering wheel
b)   steer carefully to the left
c)   steer carefully to the right
d)   brake firmly and steer to the left

Question 34 (8.34)
To correct a rear-wheel skid you should

Mark one answer
a)   apply your handbrake
b)   turn into it
c)   not turn at all
d)   turn away from it

Question 35 (4.41)
You are braking on a wet road. Your vehicle begins to skid. Your vehicle does not have anti-lock brakes. What is the FIRST thing you should do?

Mark one answer
a)   Quickly pull up the handbrake.
b)   Release the footbrake fully.
c)   Push harder on the brake pedal.
d)   Gently use the accelerator.

Question 36 (4.22)
What is the most common cause of skidding?

Mark one answer
a)   Worn tyres.
b)   Driver error.
c)   Other vehicles.
d)   Pedestrians.

Question 37 (5.92)
A driver pulls out of a side road in front of you. You have to brake hard. You should.

Mark one answer
a) overtake as soon as possible
b) sound your horn to show your annoyance
c) ignore the error and stay calm
d) flash your lights to show your annoyance

Question 38 (2.50)
You should ONLY flash your head lamps to other road users

Mark one answer
a) to tell them you have right of way
b) to show you are giving way
c) to let them know you are there
d) to show you are about to reverse

Question 39 (2.27)
When are you allowed to exceed the maximum speed limit?

Mark one answer
a) Between midnight and 6 am.
b) Never.
c) When overtaking.
d) When the road's clear.

Question 40 (4.68)
You are driving in a built-up area. You approach a speed hump. You should

Mark one answer
a) move across to the left-hand side of the road
b) stop and check both pavements
c) slow your vehicle right down
d) wait for any pedestrians to cross

Question 41 (10.3)
What is the meaning of this sign?

Mark one answer
a) Local speed limit applies.
b) No waiting on the carriageway.
c) National speed limit applies.
d) No entry to vehicular traffic.

Question 42 (11.155)
Which of these signs means that the national speed limit applies?

Mark one answer

Sign A   Sign B

Sign C   Sign D

Question 43 (10.10)
You see this sign ahead of you. It means

Mark one answer
a) Do not exceed 30mph after passing it
b) The minimum speed limit ahead is 30mph
c) Start to slow down to 30 mph after passing it
d) You are leaving the 30 mph limit area

Question 44 (10.11)
If you see a 30mph limit ahead this means

Mark one answer
a) the restriction applies only during the working day
b) you must not exceed this speed
c) you must keep your speed up to 30 mph
d) it is a guide. You are allowed to drive 10% faster

Question 45 (10.12)
What does a speed limit sign like this mean?

Mark one answer
a) The speed shown allows for various road and weather conditions
b) It is safe to drive at the speed shown
c) The speed shown is the advised maximum
d) You must not exceed the speed shown

Question 46 (10.14)
What does this sign mean?

Mark one answer
a) Minimum speed 30 mph.
b) End of maximum speed.
c) End of minimum speed.
d) Maximum speed 30 mph.

Question 47 (11.38)
What does this sign mean?

Mark one answer
a) Service area 30 miles ahead
b) Lay-by 30 miles ahead
c) Maximum Speed 30mph
d) Minimum speed 30mph

Question 48 (11.8)
This traffic sign means there is

Mark one answer
a) a compulsory maximum speed limit
b) an advised maximum speed limit.
c) a compulsory minimum speed limit.
d) an advised separation distance.

Question 49 (10.15)
You are driving along a street with parked vehicles on the left-hand side. For which THREE reasons must you keep your speed down?

Mark three answers
a) You may set off car alarms
b) So that oncoming traffic can see you more clearly
c) Children may run out from between the vehicles
d) Vehicles may be pulling out
e) Drivers' doors may open

Question 50 (10.5)
What is the national speed limit for cars and motorcycles on a dual carriageway?

Mark one answer
a) 30 mph
b) 70 mph
c) 50 mph
d) 60 mph

Question 51 (10.4)
What is the national speed limit on a single carriageway road for cars and motorcycles?

Mark one answer
a) 70 mph.
b) 60 mph.
c) 50 mph.
d) 30 mph.

Question 52 (3.73)
What will cause high fuel consumption?

Mark one answer
a) Poor steering control.
b) Accelerating around bends.
c) Driving in high gears.
d) Harsh braking and accelerating.

Question 53 (3.79)
Your car will use more fuel if fitted with

Mark one answer
a) a tow bar
b) a roof rack
c) an oil cooler
d) a sunroof

Question 54 (3.74)
A properly serviced vehicle will give

Mark two answers
a) Lower insurance premiums
b) You a refund on your road tax
c) Better fuel economy
d) Cleaner exhaust emissions

Question 55 (3.77)
You should avoid driving a vehicle fitted with an empty roof-rack.
Why is this ?

Mark one answer
a) It is illegal.
b) It will waste fuel.
c) It will affect your braking.
d) It will affect the suspension.

Question 56 (3.78)
A roof rack fitted to your car will

Mark one answer
a) reduce fuel consumption
b) improve the road handling
c) make your car go faster
d) increase fuel consumption

Question 57 (1.25)
You should ONLY use a hand-held telephone when

Mark one answer
a) you have stopped at a safe place
b) your vehicle has an automatic gear change
c) travelling on minor roads
d) driving at low speeds

Question 58 (1.26)
You are driving a vehicle fitted with a hand telephone. To answer the telephone you MUST

Mark one answer
a) find a safe place to stop
b) steer the car with one hand
c) be particularly careful at junctions
d) reduce your speed

Question 59 (3.31)
The main cause of brake fade is

Mark one answer
a) the brakes overheating
b) air in the brake fluid
c) oil on the brakes
d) the brakes out of adjustment.

Question 60 (3.76)
When driving a car fitted with automatic transmission what would you use 'kick down' for?

Mark one answer
a) Cruise control.
b) Quick acceleration.
c) Slow braking.
d) Fuel economy.

Question 61 (4.49)
The main benefit of having four wheel drive is to improve

Mark one answer
a) road holding
b) fuel consumption
c) stopping distances
d) passenger comfort

Question 62 (11.136)
When motorists flash their headlights at you it means

Mark one answer
a) they are warning you of their presence
b) they are giving way to you
c) there is something wrong with your vehicle
d) there is a radar speed trap ahead

Question 63 (5.63)
A single carriageway road has this sign. What's the maximum permitted speed for a car towing a trailer?

Mark one answer
a) 30 mph.
b) 40 mph.
c) 50 mph.
d) 60 mph.

Question 64 (14.16)
You plan to carry a load on a trailer. You must make sure that the load is

Mark one answer
a) properly secured
b) not heavier than the trailer
c) not overhanging the trailer
d) Covered with sheeting

Question 65 (14.18)
A trailer must stay securely hitched-up to the towing vehicle. What additional safety device can be fitted to the trailer braking system?

Mark one answer
a) Stabiliser.
b) Jockey wheel.
c) Corner steadies.
d) Breakaway cable.

Question 66 (10.13)
You are towing a small caravan on a dual carriageway. You must not exceed

Mark one answer
a) 50 mph
b) 40 mph
c) 70 mph
d) 60 mph.

Question 67 (14.21)
You are towing a caravan along a motorway. The caravan begins to swerve from side to side. What should you do?

Mark one answer
a) Ease off the accelerator slowly.
b) Steer sharply from side to side.
c) Do an emergency stop.
d) Speed up a little.

Question 68 (2.25)
You are driving at the legal speed limit. A vehicle comes up quickly behind, flashing its headlamps. You should

Mark one answer
a) allow the vehicle to overtake
b) touch the brakes to show your brake lights
c) accelerate to maintain a gap behind you
d) maintain your speed and prevent the vehicle from overtaking

Question 69 (2.28)
You are driving at the legal speed limit. A vehicle behind wants to overtake. Should you try to prevent the driver overtaking?

Mark one answer
a) Yes, because the other driver is breaking the law
b) Yes, because the other driver is acting dangerously
c) No, not at any time
d) No, unless it is safe to do so

Question 70 (4.29)
Braking distances on ice can be

Mark one answer
a) five times the normal distance
b) ten times the normal distance
c) twice the normal distance
d) seven times the normal distance

Lesson Introduction

In preparation for practical training on junctions (i.e. T Junctions, Y Junctions, Cross Roads and Roundabouts) we cover all the theory questions related to dealing with them at this stage. Therefore all the signs, signals and road markings associated with junctions are covered in this lesson. Similarly all the basic potential hazards at junctions are covered and how traffic at junctions can be controlled by traffic controllers or traffic lights.

This theory lesson would be undertaken before starting the first driving lesson on junctions. It would start before practical lesson 6 "Hazard drill and approaching junctions".

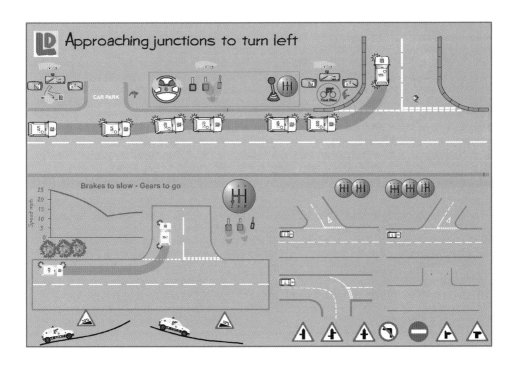

Lesson Study References

Lesson Quiz

Question 1 (2.55)
You are in a one-way street and want to turn right. You should position yourself

Mark one answer
a) in the right-hand lane
b) in either lane depending on the traffic
c) in the left-hand lane
d) just left of the centre line

Question 2 (5.24)
Why must you take extra care when turning right at this junction ?

Mark one answer
a) Road surface is poor.
b) Footpaths are narrow.
c) Road markings are faint .
d) There is reduced visibility.

Question 3 (6.11)
You are turning left into a side road. What hazards should you be especially aware of ?

Mark one answer
a) One way street.
b) Pedestrians.
c) Traffic Congestion.
d) Parked vehicles.

Question 4 (6.16)
You intend to turn right into a side road. Just before turning you should check for motorcyclists who might be

Mark one answer
a) overtaking on your left
b) following you closely
c) emerging from the side road
d) overtaking on your right

Question 5 (6.19)
You are at the front of a queue of traffic waiting to turn right into a side road. Why is it important to check your right mirror just before turning ?

Mark one answer
a) To look for pedestrians to cross.
b) To check for overtaking vehicles.
c) To make sure the side road is clear.
d) To check for emerging traffic

Question 6 (10.65)
The car ahead of you is waiting to turn right. The driver should only turn

Mark one answer
a) when the green filter arrow appears
b) when the light changes to red
c) after approaching traffic has cleared
d) when the light changes to amber

Question 7 (5.40)
You intend to turn left at the traffic lights. Just before turning you should

Mark one answer
a) check your right mirror
b) move close up to the white car
c) straddle the lanes
d) check for bicycles on your left

Question 8 (5.38)
You are driving in the left lane but want to turn right at the traffic lights. You should

Mark one answer
a) check your mirrors, signal and move to the right
b) weave into the middle and then to the right lane
c) drive up to the lights then turn right
d) stay in your lane and find another way back

Question 9 (10.66)
While driving, you intend to turn left into a minor road. On the approach you should

Mark one answer
a) keep just left of the middle of the road
b) keep in the middle of the road
c) swing out wide just before turning
d) keep well to the left of the road.

Question 10 (11.39)
Which of these signs means turn left ahead?

Mark one answer

a) 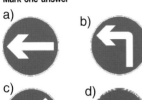 b)

c)  d)

Question 11 (5.41)
You should reduce your speed when driving along this road because

Mark one answer
a) there is a staggered junction ahead
b) there is a low bridge ahead
c) there is a change in the road surface
d) the road ahead narrows

Question 12 (6.64)
Why should you look particularly for motorcyclist and cyclists at junctions ?

Mark one answer
a) They may want to turn into the side road.
b) They may slow down to let you turn.
c) They are harder to see.
d) They might not see you turn.

Question 13 (10.52)
Signals are normally given by direction indicators and

Mark one answer
a) brake lights
b) side lights
c) fog lights
d) interior lights.

Question 14 (11.137)
Why should you make sure that you have cancelled your indicators after turning?

Mark one answer
a) To avoid flattening the battery.
b) To avoid misleading other road users.
c) To avoid dazzling other road users.
d) To avoid damage to the indicator relay.

Question 15 (11.138)
You are waiting at a T-junction. A vehicle is coming from the right with the left signal flashing. What should you do?

Mark one answer
a) Move out and accelerate hard
b) Wait until the vehicle starts to turn in
c) Move out slowly
d) Pull out before the vehicle reaches the junction

Question 16 (11.125)
The driver of the car in front is giving this arm signal. What does it mean?

Mark one answer
a) The driver is slowing down.
b) The driver intends to turn right.
c) The driver wishes to overtake.
d) The driver intends to turn left.

Question 17 (11.126)
The driver of this car is giving a hand signal. What is he about to do?

Mark one answer
a) Turn to the left.
b) Turn to the right.
c) Go straight ahead.
d) Let pedestrians cross.

Question 18 (11.127)
Which arm signal tells a following vehicle you intend to turn left?

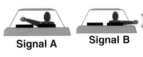

Signal A   Signal B
Signal C   Signal D

Mark one answer
a) Signal A
b) Signal B
c) Signal C
d) Signal D

Question 19 (11.133)
You want to turn right at a junction but you think that your indicators cannot be seen clearly. What should you do?

Mark one answer
a) Keep well over to the right
b) Get out and check if your indicators can be seen
c) Give an arm signal as well as an indicator signal
d) Stay in the left-hand lane

Question 20 (11.128)
How should you give an arm signal to turn left.

Mark one answer

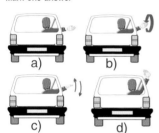

a)   b)

c)   d)

Question 21 (5.3)
What does this signal, from a police officer, mean to oncoming traffic?

Mark one answer
a) Go ahead.
b) Stop.
c) Turn left.
d) Turn right.

Question 22 (11.124)
You approach a junction. The traffic lights are not working. A police officer gives this signal. You should

Mark one answer
a) Turn right only
b) Stop level with the officer's arm
c) Turn left only
d) Stop at the stop line

Question 23 (5.39)
When the traffic lights change to green the white car should

Mark one answer
a) wait for the cyclist to pull away
b) move off quickly and turn in front of the cyclist
c) move close up to the cyclist to beat the lights
d) sound the horn to warn the cyclist

Question 24 (11.96)
You see this traffic light ahead. Which light(s) will come on next?

Mark one answer
a) Red alone
b) Green alone
c) Green and amber together
d) Red and amber together

Question 25 (11.97)
You are approaching a red traffic light. The signal will change from red to

Mark one answer
a) red and amber, then green
b) green and amber, then green
c) green, then amber
d) amber, then green

Question 26 (11.98)
A red traffic light means

Mark one answer
a) proceed with caution
b) you must stop and wait behind the stop line
c) you should stop unless turning left
d) stop if you are able to brake safely

Question 27 (11.99)
At traffic lights, amber on its own means

Mark one answer
a) go if no pedestrians are crossing
b) stop at the stop line
c) prepare to go
d) go if the way is clear

Question 28 (11.100)

A red traffic light means

Mark one answer

a) you must slow down and prepare to stop if traffic has started to cross

b) you must stop behind the white stop line

c) you may turn left if it is safe to do so

d) you may drive straight on if there is no other traffic

Question 29 (11.101)

You are approaching traffic lights. Red and amber are showing. This means

Mark one answer

a) wait for the green light before you pass the lights

b) pass the lights if the road is clear

c) there is a fault with the lights - take care

d) the lights are about to change to red

Question 30 (11.102)

You are at a junction controlled by traffic lights. When should you NOT proceed at green?

Mark one answer

a) When your exit from the junction is blocked

b) When you intend to turn right

c) When you think the lights may be about to change

d) When pedestrians are waiting to cross

Question 31 (11.103)

You are in the left-hand lane at traffic lights. You are waiting to turn left. At which of these lights must you NOT move on?

Signal A

Signal B

Signal C

Signal D

Mark one answer

a) Signal A

b) Signal B

c) Signal C

d) Signal D

Question 32 (11.104)

What does this sign mean?

Mark one answer

a) Amber signal out of order

b) New traffic lights ahead

c) Temporary traffic lights ahead

d) Traffic lights out of order

Question 33 (11.106)

When traffic lights are out of order, who has priority?

Mark one answer

a) Traffic going straight on.

b) Traffic turning right.

c) Nobody.

d) Traffic turning left.

Question 34 (11.13)

At this junction, when the green signal is showing, you must

Mark one answer

a) not go ahead

b) turn right

c) turn left

d) not turn right

Question 35 (11.105)
You see this sign at a crossroads. You should

Mark one answer
a) maintain the same speed
b) drive on with great care
c) find another route
d) telephone the police

Question 36 (5.47)
At this blind junction you must stop

Mark one answer
a) behind the line, then edge forward to see clearly
b) beyond the line at a point where you can see clearly
c) only if there is traffic on the main road
d) only if you are turning to the right

Question 37 (5.48)
When must you stop at this junction ?

Mark one answer
a) During rush hour only.
b) Only when the area is busy.
c) When turning right only.
d) At all times.

Question 38 (11.32)
What should you do when you see this sign?

Mark one answer
a) Stop, ONLY if children are waiting to cross
b) Stop, even if the road is clear
c) Stop, ONLY if the traffic is approaching
d) Stop, ONLY if a red light is showing

Question 39 (11.34)
What shape is a stop sign at a junction?

Mark one answer

Sign A   Sign B

Sign C   Sign D

Question 40 (11.36)
Which shape of traffic sign means that you must stop?

Mark one answer

Sign A   Sign B

Sign C   Sign D

Question 41 (11.119)
At a junction there is a stop sign with a solid white line on the road surface. Why?

Mark one answer
a) Visibility along the major road is restricted
b) It is a busy junction
c) Speed on the major road is de-restricted
d) There are hazard warning lines in the centre of the road

Question 42 (11.35)
At a junction you see this sign partly covered by snow. What does it mean?

Mark one answer
a) Cross roads
b) Give way
c) Stop
d) Turn right

Question 43 (11.37)
Which shape is used for a Give Way sign ?

Mark one answer

Sign A   Sign B

Sign C   Sign D

67

Question 44 (11.116)
This marking appears on the road just before a

Mark one answer
a)   no entry sign
b)   give way sign
c)   stop sign
d)   no through road sign

Question 45 (11.52)
What does this sign mean?

Mark one answer
a)   Turn left ahead.
b)   T-junction.
c)   No through road.
d)   Give way.

Question 46 (2.47)
At unmarked junctions where tram lines cross over roads, who has priority?

Mark one answer
a)   Cars.
b)   Motorcycles.
c)   Trams.
d)   Buses.

Question 47 (10.58)
At a crossroads there are no signs or road markings. Two vehicles approach. Which has priority?

Mark one answer
a)   The vehicle travelling the fastest
b)   The vehicle on the widest road
c)   Neither vehicle
d)   Vehicles approaching from the right

Question 48 (10.59)
At a crossroads with no road markings who has priority?

Mark one answer
a)   Traffic from the left.
b)   Traffic from the right.
c)   Nobody.
d)   Traffic from ahead.

Question 49 (10.60)
Who has priority at an unmarked crossroads?

Mark one answer
a)   No one
b)   The driver on the wider road
c)   The driver of the larger vehicle
d)   The driver who is going faster

Question 50 (10.62)
You are intending to turn right at a junction. An oncoming driver is also turning right. It will normally be safer to

Mark one answer
a)   carry on and turn at the next junction instead
b)   hold back and wait for the other driver to turn first
c)   keep the other vehicle to your RIGHT and turn behind it (offside to offside)
d)   keep the other vehicle to your LEFT and turn in front of it (nearside to nearside)

Question 51 (11.54)
What does this sign mean?

Mark one answer
a)   Crossroads.
b)   Level crossing with gate.
c)   Level crossing without gate.
d)   Ahead only.

Question 52 (5.11)
What should the driver of the grey car (arrowed) do?

Mark one answer
a)   Wait in the same place until the lights are green
b)   Wait until the lights are red then cross
c)   Cross if the way is clear
d)   Reverse out of the box junction

Question 53 (8.73)
When may you wait in a box junction?

Mark one answer
a)   When you are stationary in a qeue of traffic.
b)   When approaching a pelican crossing.
c)   When approaching a zebra crossing.
d)   When oncoming traffic prevents you turning right.

Question 54 (10.67)
You may only enter a box junction when

Mark one answer
a) there are less than two vehicles in front of you
b) the traffic lights show green
c) your exit road is clear
d) you need to turn left.

Question 55 (10.68)
You may wait in a yellow box junction when

Mark one answer
a) oncoming traffic is preventing you from turning right
b) you are in a queue of traffic turning left
c) you are in a queue of traffic to go ahead
d) you are on a roundabout.

Question 56 (10.69)
You want to turn right at a box junction. You should

Mark one answer
a) wait in the box junction if your exit is clear
b) wait before the junction until it is clear of all traffic
c) drive on: you cannot turn right at box junction
d) drive slowly into the box junction when signalled by oncoming traffic.

Question 57 (6.94)
You are approaching a roundabout. There are horses just ahead of you. You should

Mark two answers
a) be prepared to stop
b) treat them like any other vehicle
c) give them plenty of room
d) accelerate past as quickly as possible
e) sound your horn as a warning

Question 58 (10.53)
When going straight ahead at a roundabout you should

Mark one answer
a) indicate left before leaving the roundabout
b) not indicate at any time
c) indicate right when approaching the roundabout
d) indicate left when approaching the roundabout

Question 59 (10.55)
You are going straight ahead at a roundabout. How should you signal?

Mark one answer
a) Signal left just after you pass the exit before the one you will take
b) Signal left on the approach to the roundabout and keep the signal on until you leave
c) Signal left as you leave the exit of the roundabout
d) Signal right on the approach and then left to leave the roundabout

Question 60 (10.18)
Which three of the following may take an unusual course at roundabouts ?

Mark three answers
a) Horse riders.
b) Milk floats.
c) Delivery vans.
d) Long vehicles.
e) Estate cars.
f) Cyclists.

Question 61 (11.55)
What does this sign mean?

Mark one answer
a) Ring road.
b) Mini-roundabout.
c) Restriction ends.
d) Roundabout.

Question 62 (11.95)
Which exit from this roundabout leads onto a dual carriageway ?

Mark one answer
a) First
b) Second
c) Third
d) Fourth

Question 63 (11.120)
You see a line across the road at a roundabout. What does it mean?

Mark one answer
a) You have right of way
b) Give way to traffic from the right
c) Stop at the line
d) Traffic from the left has right of way

69

Question 64 (11.40)
At a mini-roundabout you should

Mark one answer
a) give way to traffic from the right.
b) give way to traffic from the left
c) give way to traffic from the right and left
d) stop even when clear.

Question 65 (11.121)
Where whould you find this road marking?

Mark one answer
a) At a railway crossing.
b) At a junction.
c) On the motorway.
d) On a pedestrian crossing.

Question 66 (11.41)
What does this sign mean ?

Mark one answer
a) Buses turning.
b) Ring road.
c) Mini roundabout.
d) Keep right.

Question 67 (4.51)
You are at a junction with limited visibility. You should

Mark one answer
a) be ready to move off quickly
b) inch forward, looking to the left
c) inch forward, looking to the right
d) inch forward, looking both ways

Question 68 (6.18)
You want to turn right from a junction but your view is restricted by parked vehicles. What should you do?

Mark one answer
a) Sound your horn and pull out if there is no reply
b) Stop, them move forward until you have a clear view
c) Stop, get out and look along the main road to check
d) Move out quickly, but be prepared to stop

Question 69 (7.5)
You are waiting to emerge left from a minor road. A large vehicle is approaching from the right. You have time to turn, but you should wait. Why?

Mark one answer
a) The large vehicle can easily hide an overtaking vehicle.
b) The large vehicle can turn suddenly.
c) The large vehicle is difficult to steer in a straight line.
d) The large vehicle can easily hide vehicles from the left.

Question 70 (11.11)
What does this sign mean?

Mark one answer
a) Bend to the right.
b) Road on the right closed.
c) No traffic from the right.
d) No right turn.

Lesson Introduction

To begin with your driving lessons will be conducted on very quite roads. However, after about 6 lessons you will begin to start to meet other road users. Hence, during this lesson you will cover all the theory questions that relate to the basics of dealing with traffic.

This theory lesson would be undertaken before driving lesson 7 of the Learner Driving practical programme (i.e. "Emerging fron T and Y Junctions").

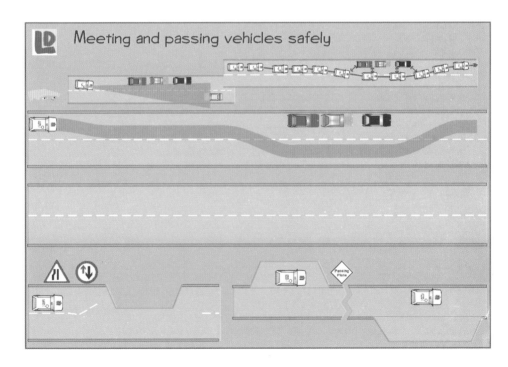

Meeting and passing vehicles safely

Lesson Study References

Q. 01 Cycles (HC Rule 240 R 278) (DM Page 121)
Q. 02 Cyclists (HC Rule 52 R 187) (DM Page 209)
Q. 03 Cyclists (HC Page 83 TN 21 R 163) (DM Page 169)
Q. 04 Cyclists (HC Page 60) (KYTS Page 32)
Q. 05 Cyclists (HC Page 83 TN 21 R 163) (DM Page 169)
Q. 06 Cyclists (HC Rule 52 R 189) (DM Page 209)
Q. 07 Cyclists (HC Page 83 TN 21 R 163/187)
       (DM Page 169)
Q. 08 Cyclists & Pedestrians (HC Page 59)
       (KYTS Page 32)
Q. 09 Cycle Lane (HC Page 59) (KYTS Page 32)
Q. 10 Cycle Lanes (HC Rules 98/138 R 119)
Q. 11 Cycle Lanes (HC Rules 98 R 119)
Q. 12 Cycle Lanes (HC Rules 98/138 R 119)
Q. 13 Cyclists (HC Page 60) (KYTS Page 32)
Q. 14 Vulnerable (HC R 180) (DM Page 209)
Q. 15 Right Turns (HC R 156) (DM Page 198)
Q. 16 Right Turns (HC R 156) (DM Page 198)
Q. 17 Motorcyclists (HC Rules 52/107 Page 209 R 187)
Q. 18 Motorcyclists (HC Rule 30 R 69)
Q. 19 Motorcyclists (HC Rule 107 R's 146/187)
Q. 20 Motorcyclists (HC Rule 107 Page 209 R's 146/187)
Q. 21 Motorcyclists (HC Rule 52 Page 209 R's 180/187)
Q. 22 Motorcyclists (HC Rule 30 R 69)
Q. 23 Motorcyclists (HC Rule 30 R 69)
Q. 24 Motorcyclists (HC Page 209 R 188)
Q. 25 Motorcyclists (HC Rule 107 Page 209 R 187)
Q. 26 Motorcyclists (HC R 187)
Q. 27 Motorcyclists (HC R 187)
Q. 28 Motorcyclists (HC Page 209)
Q. 29 Approaching Motorcyclist (HC Rule 30 R 69)
Q. 30 Motorcyclists (HC Page 84 TN 28 R 189)
Q. 31 Pull Out (HC Page 81 TN 13 R 125)
Q. 32 Pull Out (HC Page 81 TN 10 R 125)
Q. 33 CarDoors (HC Page 82 TN 16 R 130)
Q. 34 Car Emerging (HC Page 80 TN 4)
Q. 35 Inexperienced (HC Page 83 TN 23 R 193)

Q. 36 Large Vehicle (HC Page 83 TN 27 R 196)
Q. 37 Slow Lorry (HC Page 63) (KYTS Page 94)
Q. 38 Large Vehicle Markings (HC Page 66)
Q. 39 Long Vehicles (HC Rule 127 R 163)
Q. 40 High Vehicles (HC Page 58) (KYTS Page 22)
Q. 41 Bus Lanes (HC Rule 97 R 120) (DM Page 94)
Q. 42 Buses (HC Rule 79 R 198) (DM Page 200)
Q. 43 Buses (HC Rule 79 R 198) (DM Page 200)
Q. 44 School Bus (HC Page 66 R 185)
Q. 45 School Bus (HC Page 66 R 185)
Q. 46 School Bus (HC Page 66 R 185)
Q. 47 Buses (HC Rule 79 R 198) (DM Page 200)
Q. 48 Buses (HC Rule 79 R 198) (DM Page 200)
Q. 49 Bus Lanes (HC Page 59) (KYTS Page 30)
Q. 50 Bus Lanes (HC Page 59) (KYTS Page 30)
Q. 51 Trams (HC R 273) (KYTS Page 29)
Q. 52 Trams (DM Page 121)
Q. 53 Trams (HC R 199) (DM Pages 120/138)
Q. 54 Trams (HC Page 59) (DM Page 121)
       (KYTS Page 29)
Q. 55 Trams (HC Page 59) (DM Page 121)
       (KYTS Page 29)
Q. 56 Trams (HC Page 59) (DM Page 138)
       (KYTS Page 29)
Q. 57 Trams (HC Page 60)
Q. 58 Compulsory Stop (HC Page 70 R's 89/151/260)
Q. 59 CompulsoryStop (HC Page 70 R's 89/151/260)
Q. 60 Police Vehicles (HC Rule 78 R 89)
Q. 61 Police Vehicles (HC Rule 78 R 89)
Q. 62 Warning Sign (HC Pages 59/60)
Q. 63 Trailers (HC Page 94 TN 93 R 74) (DM Page 310)
Q. 64 Trailers (HC Page 94 TN 93 R 74) (DM Page 313)
Q. 65 Trailers (HC Page 94 TN 93 R 74) (DM Page 313)
Q. 66 Trailers (HC Pages 53/71 R's 103/239)
Q. 67 Caravans (HC R 74) (DM Page 310)
Q. 68 Caravans (DM Page 310)
Q. 69 Caravans (HC Page 94 TN 93 R 74)
       (DM Page 313)
Q. 70 Caravans (DM Page 310)

72

Lesson Quiz

Question 1 (2.46)
On a road where trams operate, which of these vehicles will be most at risk from the tram rails?

Mark one answer
a) Cars.
b) Cycles.
c) Buses.
d) Lorries.

Question 2 (5.4)
What is the main hazard shown in this picture?

Mark one answer
a) Vehicles turning right
b) Parked cars around the corner
c) The cyclist crossing the road
d) Vehicles doing U-turns

Question 3 (6.58)
You are driving behind two cyclists. They approach a roundabout in the left-hand lane. In which direction should you expect the cyclists to go?

Mark one answer
a) Any direction
b) Right
c) Straight ahead
d) Left

Question 4 (6.31)
What does this sign tell you?

Mark one answer
a) No cycling.
b) Cycle route ahead.
c) Route for cycles only.
d) End of cycle route.

Question 5 (6.57)
You are coming up to a roundabout. A cyclist is signalling to turn right. What should you do?

Mark one answer
a) Give a horn warning
b) Overtake on the right
c) Give the cyclist plenty of room
d) Signal the cyclist to move across

Question 6 (5.14)
What is the main hazard a driver should be aware of when following this cyclist?

Mark one answer
a) The cyclist may swerve out into the road.
b) The cyclist may wish to turn right at the end of the road.
c) The cyclist may move into the left gap and dismount.
d) The contents of the cyclists carrier may fall onto the road.

Question 7 (6.59)
You are approaching the roundabout and see the cyclist signal right. Why is the cyclist keeping to the left?

Mark one answer
a) The cyclist is going to turn left instead
b) The cyclist is slower and more vulnerable.
c) It is a quicker route for the cyclist.
d) The cyclist thinks The Highway Code does not apply to bicycles

Question 8 (6.45)
What does this sign mean ?

Mark one answer
a) No route for pedestrians and cyclists.
b) A route for pedestrians only.
c) A route for cyclists only.
d) A route for pedestrians and cyclists.

Question 9 (6.54)
What does this sign mean ?

Mark one answer
a) Contra-flow pedal cycle lane.
b) With-flow pedal cycle lane.
c) Pedal cycles and buses only.
d) No pedal cycles or buses.

Question 10 (10.44)
You are driving on a road that has a cycle lane. The lane is marked by a solid white line. This means that

Mark one answer
a) you must not drive in the lane unless it is unavoidable
b) the lane can be used for parking your vehicle
c) you can drive in the lane at any time
d) the lane must be used by motorcyclists in heavy traffic.

Question 11 (10.45)
You are driving along a road that has a cycle lane. The lane is marked by an unbroken white line. This means that during its period of operation

Mark one answer
a) the lane may be used for parking your car
b) you may drive in that lane at any time
c) the lane may be used when necessary
d) you must not drive in that lane

Question 12 (10.46)
A cycle lane is marked by an unbroken white line. You must not drive or park in it

Mark one answer
a) at any time
b) during the rush hour
c) if a cyclist is using it
d) during its period of operation

Question 13 (11.57)
What does this sign mean?

Mark one answer
a) Walking is not allowed
b) Bicycles are not allowed
c) You are approaching a cycle route
d) Cyclists must dismount

Question 14 (6.75)
At road junctions which of the following are most vulnerable?

Mark three answers
a) Cyclists.
b) Motorcyclists.
c) Pedestrians.
d) Car drivers.
e) Lorry drivers.

Question 15 (6.77)
You want to turn right from a main road into a side road. Just before turning you should

Mark one answer
a) cancel your right-turn signal
b) select first gear
c) check for traffic overtaking on your right
d) stop and set the handbrake.

Question 16 (6.80)
You are driving on a main road. You intend to turn right into a side road. Just before turning you should

Mark one answer
a) adjust your interior mirror
b) flash your headlamps
c) steer over to the left
d) check for traffic overtaking on your offside.

Question 17 (6.65)
You are waiting to come out of a side road. Why should you watch carefully for motorcycles?

Mark one answer
a) Motorcycles are small and hard to see
b) Police patrols often use motorcycles
c) Motorcycles are usually faster than cars
d) Motorcycles have right of way

Question 18 (6.67)
In daylight, an approaching motorcyclist is using a dipped headlight. Why?

Mark one answer
a) So that the rider can be seen more easily.
b) To stop the battery over-charging.
c) To improve the rider's vision.
d) The rider is inviting you to proceed.

Question 19 (6.66)
Where should you take particular care to look out for motorcyclists and cyclists?

Mark one answer
a) On one-way streets
b) At junctions
c) At zebra crossings
d) On dual carriageways

Question 20 (6.68)
Where in particular should you look out for motorcyclists?

Mark one answer
a) In a filling station
b) Near a service area
c) When entering a car park
d) At a road junction

Question 21 (6.69)
Motorcycle riders are vulnerable because they

Mark one answer
a) are easy for other road users to see
b) are difficult for other road users to see
c) are likely to have breakdowns
d) cannot give arm signals.

Question 22 (6.70)
Motorcyclists should wear bright clothing mainly because

Mark one answer
a) they must do so by law
b) it helps keep them cool in summer
c) the colours are popular
d) drivers often do not see them.

Question 23 (6.71)
Motorcyclists ride in daylight with their headlights switched on because

Mark one answer
a) it is a legal requirement
b) there's a speed trap ahead
c) they need to be seen
d) there are speed humps ahead.

Question 24 (6.74)
Motorcyclists will often look round over their right shoulder just before turning right. This is because

Mark one answer
a) they need to listen for following traffic
b) motorcycles do not have mirrors
c) looking around helps them balance as they turn
d) they need to check for traffic in their blind area.

Question 25 (6.76)
When emerging from a side road into a queue of traffic which vehicles can be especially difficult to see?

Mark one answer
a) Motorcycles.
b) Tractors.
c) Milk floats.
d) Cars.

Question 26 (6.79)
Which of the following are hazards motorcyclists present in queues of traffic?

Mark three answers
a) Cutting in just in front of you.
b) Riding in single file.
c) Passing very close to your car.
d) Riding with their headlamp on dipped beam.
e) Filtering between the lanes.

Question 27 (6.82)
You are driving in slow-moving queues of traffic. Just before changing lane you should

Mark one answer
a) sound the horn
b) look for motorcyclists filtering through the traffic
c) give a 'slowing down' arm signal
d) change down to first gear.

Question 28 (6.83)
Which of the following are a major cause of motorcycle collisions?

Mark one answer
a) Car drivers.
b) Moped riders.
c) Sunny weather conditions.
d) Traffic lights.

Question 29 (5.42)
An approaching motorcyclist is easier to see when

Mark three answers
a) the rider is wearing bright clothing
b) the rider has a white helmet
c) the headlight is on
d) the motorcycle is moving slowly
e) the motorcyclist is moving quickly
f) the rider has a passenger

Question 30 (7.1)
The road is wet. Why might a motorcyclist steer round drain covers on a bend?

Mark one answer
a) To help judge the bend using the drain covers as marker points
b) To prevent the motorcycle sliding on the metal drain covers
c) To avoid splashing pedestrians on the pavement
d) To avoid puncturing the tyres on the edge of the drain covers

Question 31 (2.52)
A vehicle pulls out in front of you at a junction. What should you do?

Mark one answer
a) Slow down and be ready to stop
b) Flash your headlights and drive up close behind
c) Accelerate past it immediately
d) Swerve past it and blow your horn

Question 32 (5.93)
A car driver pulls out causing you to brake. You should

Mark one answer
a) keep calm and not retaliate
b) overtake and sound your horn
c) drive close behind and sound your horn
d) flag the driver down and explain the mistake.

Question 33 (5.13)
What are Two main hazards a driver should be aware of when driving along this street?

Mark two answers
a) Lack of road markings
b) The headlights on parked cars being switched on
c) Children running out from between vehicles
d) Glare from the sun
e) Large goods vehicles
f) Car doors opening suddenly

Question 34 (5.15)
The driver of which car has caused a hazard?

Mark one answer
a) Car A
b) Car B
c) Car C
d) Car D

Question 35 (6.100)
How would you react to other drivers who appear to be inexperienced?

Mark one answer
a) Sound your horn to warn them of your presence.
b) Be patient and prepared for them to react more slowly.
c) Flash your headlights to indicate that it's safe for them to proceed.
d) Overtake them as soon as possible.

Question 36 (2.18)
You are driving behind a large goods vehicle. It signals left but steers to the right. You should

Mark one answer
a) slow down and let the vehicle turn
b) drive on, keeping to the left
c) overtake on the right of it
d) hold your speed and sound your horn

Question 37 (5.1)
You see this sign on the rear of a slow-moving lorry that you want to pass. It is travelling in the middle lane of a three lane motorway. You should

Mark one answer
a) cautiously approach the lorry then pass on either side
b) follow the lorry until you can leave the motorway
c) wait on the hard shoulder until the lorry has stopped
d) approach with care and keep to the left of the lorry.

Question 38 (7.11)
You are following a large vehicle. Side and end markers are being displayed. This means the load

Mark one answer
a) is higher than normal
b) may be flammable
c) is in two parts
d) overhangs at the rear

Question 39 (10.54)
Which vehicle might have to use a different course to normal at roundabouts?

Mark one answer
a) Sports car.
b) Van.
c) Estate car.
d) Long vehicle.

Question 40 (11.15)
Which type of vehicle does this sign apply to?

Mark one answer
a) Wide vehicles.
b) Long vehicles.
c) High vehicles.
d) Heavy vehicles.

Question 41 (2.49)
A bus lane on your left shows no times of its operation. This means it is

Mark one answer
a) not in operation at all
b) only in operation at peak times
c) in operation 24 hours a day
d) only in operation in daylight hours

Question 42 (2.48)
A bus is stopped at a bus stop ahead of you. Its right-hand indicator is flashing. You should

Mark one answer
a) slow down and give way if it is safe to do so
b) slow down and then sound your horn
c) flash your headlights and slow down
d) sound your horn and keep going

Question 43 (5.17)
What is the main hazard the driver of the red car (arrowed) should be most aware of?

Mark one answer
a) Oncoming vehicles will assume the driver is turning right
b) The bus may move out into the road
c) The black car may stop suddenly
d) Glare from the sun may affect the drivers vision

Question 44 (5.27)
The yellow sign on this vehicle indicates this is

Mark one answer
a) a vehicle broken down
b) a school bus
c) an ice cream van
d) a private ambulance

Question 45 (6.38)
Where would you see this sign?

Mark one answer
a) In the window of a car taking children to school.
b) At the side of the road.
c) At playground areas.
d) On the rear of a school bus or coach.

Question 46 (6.39)
Where would you see this sign?

Mark one answer
a) On the approach to a school crossing.
b) At a playground entrance.
c) On a school bus.
d) At a 'pedestrians only' area.

Question 47 (7.25)
When you approach a bus signalling to move off from a bus stop you should

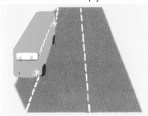

Mark one answer
a) allow it to pull away if it is safe to do so
b) signal left and wave the bus on
c) get past before it moves
d) flash your head lamps as you approach

Question 48 (7.24)
You are driving in town. Ahead of you a bus is at a bus stop. Which two of the following should you do ?

Mark two answers
a) Be prepared to give way if the bus suddenly moves off.
b) Continue at the same speed but sound your horn as a warning.
c) Watch carefully for the sudden appearance of pedestrians.
d) Pass the bus as quickly as you possibly can.

Question 49 (11.47)
What does this sign mean?

Mark one answer
a) Bus station on the right.
b) Contraflow bus lane.
c) With-flow bus lane.
d) Give way to buses.

Question 50 (11.48)
What does this sign mean?

Mark one answer
a) With-flow bus and cycle lane.
b) Contraflow bus and cycle lane.
c) No buses and cycles allowed.
d) No waiting for buses and cycles.

Question 51 (2.44)
Diamond-shaped signs give
instructions to

Mark one answer
a) tram drivers
b) bus drivers
c) lorry drivers
d) taxi drivers.

Question 52 (7.22)
You're driving along a road and you
see this signal. It means

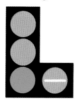

Mark one answer
a) cars must stop
b) trams must stop
c) both trams and cars must stop
d) both trams and cars can continue.

Question 53 (7.21)
As a driver, why should you be more
careful where trams operate ?

Mark two answers
a) Because they do not have a horn.
b) Because they do not stop for cars.
c) Because they are silent.
d) Because they cannot steer to
   avoid you.
e) Because they do not have lights.

Question 54 (11.14)
What does this sign mean?

Mark one answer
a) Route for trams only.
b) Route for buses only.
c) Parking for buses only.
d) Parking for trams only.

Question 55 (11.43)
What does this sign mean?

Mark one answer
a) Route for trams.
b) Give way to trams.
c) Route for buses.
d) Give way to buses.

Question 56 (11.63)
What does this sign mean?

Mark one answer
a) Wait at the barriers.
b) Wait at the crossroads.
c) Give way to trams.
d) Give way to farm vehicles.

Question 57 (11.75)
What does this sign mean?

Mark one answer
a) No trams ahead.
b) Oncoming trams.
c) Trams crossing ahad.
d) Trams only.

Question 58 (10.70)
On which THREE occasions MUST
you stop your vehicle?

Mark three answers
a) When signalled to do so by a
   police officer
b) At a junction with double broken
   white lines
c) At a pelican crossing when the
   amber light is flashing and no
   pedestrians are crossing
d) At a red traffic light
e) When involved in an accident

Question 59 (10.71)
You MUST stop when signalled to do
so by which THREE of these?

Mark three answers
a) A pedestrian
b) A red traffic light
c) A bus driver
d) A school crossing patrol
e) A police officer

Question 60 (11.122)
How will a police officer in a patrol
vehicle get you to stop?

Mark one answer
a) Pull alongside you, use the siren
   and wave you to stop
b) Flash the headlights indicate left
   and point to the left
c) Wait until you stop, then approach
   you
d) Use the siren, overtake, cut in
   front and stop

Question 61 (11.123)
There is a police car following you.
The police officer flashes the
headlights and points to the left. What
should you do?

Mark one answer
a) Stop immediately
b) Move over to the left
c) Pull up on the left
d) Turn next left

Question 62 (11.56)
Which FOUR of these would be
indicated by a triangular road sign

Mark four answers
a) Ahead only
b) Minimum Speed
c) Children crossing
d) Road narrows
e) T-junction
f) Low bridge

Question 63 (14.13)
You should load a trailer so that the
weight is

Mark one answer
a) evenly distributed
b) mostly at the rear
c) mostly over the nearside
d) wheel mainly at the front

Question 64 (14.19)
If a trailer swerves or snakes when you
are towing it you should

Mark one answer
a) brake hard and hold the pedal
   down
b) let go of the steering wheel and let
   it correct itself
c) increase your speed as quickly as
   possible
d) ease off the accelerator and
   reduce your speed

Question 65 (14.23)
You are towing a trailer and experience
snaking. How would you reduce it?

Mark one answer
a) Ease off the accelerator slowly.
b) Press the accelerator firmly.
c) Steer sharply.
d) Brake hard.

Question 66 (14.25)
You are towing a small trailer on a busy
three-lane motorway. All the lanes are
open. You must

Mark two answers
a) not exceed 60 mph
b) not overtake
c) have a stabilizer fitted
d) use only the left and centre lanes.

Question 67 (14.17)
Before towing a caravan you should
ensure that heavy items in it are loaded

Mark one answer
a) as high as possible, mainly over
   the axle(s)
b) as low as possible, mainly over
   the axle(s)
c) as low as possible, forward of the
   axle(s)
d) as high as possible, forward of the
   axle(s).

Question 68 (14.20)
Are passengers allowed to ride in a
caravan that is being towed?

Mark one answer
a) Yes.
b) No.
c) Only if all the seats in the towing
   vehicle are full.
d) Only if a stabilizer is fitted.

Question 69 (14.24)
How can you stop a caravan snaking
from side to side?

Mark one answer
a) Slow down very gradually
b) Accelerate to increase your speed
c) Turn the steering wheel slowly to
   each side
d) Stop as quickly as you can

Question   70 (14.15)
You are planning to tow a caravan.
Which of these will mostly help to aid
the vehicle handling?

Mark one answer
a)   A jockey- wheel fitted to the
      towbar.
b)   Power steering fitted to the towing
      vehicle.
c)   Anti-lock brakes fitted to the
      towing vehicle.
d)   A stabiliser fitted to the towbar.

Lesson Introduction

By lesson 8 you will begin to meet more and more traffic. Gradually, as the amount of traffic increases you will need to consider how to deal with slower and faster moving vehicles. Hence, during this lesson you will cover all the theory questions that relate to following and overtaking other traffic.

This theory lesson would be undertaken before driving lesson 8 of the Learner Driving practical programme (i.e. "Crossroads").

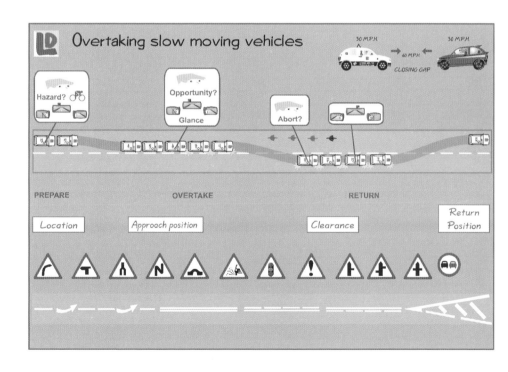

Lesson Study References

Lesson Quiz

Question 1 (1.18)
When following a large vehicle you should keep well back because

Mark one answer
a) it allows the driver to see you in his mirrors
b) it helps the large vehicle to stop more easily
c) it allows you to corner more quickly
d) it helps you keep out of the wind.

Question 2 (2.16)
Following a large goods vehicle too closely is dangerous because

Mark one answer
a) your field of vision is seriously reduced
b) slipstreaming will reduce wind effect
c) your engine will overheat
d) your brakes need a constant cooling effect.

Question 3 (2.17)
You are following this lorry. You should keep well back from it to

Mark one answer
a) give you a good view of the road ahead
b) stop following traffic from rushing through the junction
c) prevent traffic behind you from overtaking
d) allow you to hurry through the traffic lights if they change

Question 4 (7.6)
You are following a large articulated vehicle. It is going to turn left into a narrow road. What action should you take?

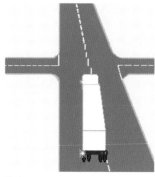

Mark one answer
a) Be prepared to stop behind
b) Overtake quickly before the lorry moves out
c) Move out and overtake on the offside
d) Pass on the left as the vehicle moves out

Question 5 (7.29)
You are following a large lorry on a wet road. Spray makes it difficult to see. You should

Mark one answer
a) drop back until you can see better
b) keep close to the lorry, away from the spray
c) speed up and overtake quickly
d) put your headlights on full beam

Question 6 (7.7)
You are following a long vehicle. It approaches a crossroads and signals left, but moves out to the right. You should

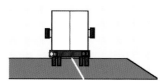

Mark one answer
a) get closer in order to pass it quickly
b) overtake as it starts to slow down
c) assume the signal is wrong and it is really turning right
d) stay well back and give it room

Question 7 (7.9)
You are following a long vehicle approaching a crossroads. The driver signals right but moves close to the left-hand kerb. What should you do?

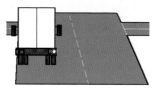

Mark one answer
a) Overtake on the right-hand side
b) Report the driver to the police
c) Wait behind the long vehicle
d) Warn the driver of wrong signal

Question 8 (7.10)
You are approaching a mini-roundabout. The long vehicle in front is signalling left but positioned over to the right. You should

Mark one answer
a)   follow the same course as the lorry
b)   sound your horn
c)   overtake on the left
d)   keep well back

Question 9 (7.23)
You are travelling behind a bus that pulls up at a bus stop. What should you do?

Mark two answers
a)   Accelerate past the bus sounding your horn.
b)   Watch carefully for pedestrians.
c)   Be ready to give way to the bus.
d)   Pull in closely behind the bus.

Question 10 (2.31)
You are driving at night on an unlit road following a slower moving vehicle. You should

Mark one answer
a)   flash your headlights
b)   use dipped beam headlights
c)   switch off your headlights
d)   use full beam headlights

Question 11 (6.103)
You are following a learner driver who stalls at a junction. You should

Mark one answer
a)   be patient as you expect them to make mistakes
b)   drive up close behind and flash your headlamps
c)   start to rev your engine if they take too long to re-start
d)   immediately steer around them and drive on

Question 12 (6.42)
You are following a car driven by an elderly driver. You should

Mark one answer
a)   stay close behind and drive carefully
b)   expect the driver to drive badly
c)   flash your lights and overtake
d)   be aware that the driver's reactions may not be as fast as yours

Question 13 (6.51)
Why should you be more careful when following elderly drivers ?

Mark one answer
a)   Their passengers may be talking to them.
b)   Their reactions may be quicker than yours.
c)   Their reactions may not be as quick as yours.
d)   Their car may be very old.

Question 14 (5.22)
You are approaching this cyclist. You should

Mark one answer
a)   overtake before the cyclist gets to the junction
b)   flash your headlights at the cyclist
c)   slow down and allow the cyclist to turn
d)   overtake the cyclist on the left hand side

Question 15 (5.30)
You are behind this cyclist. When the traffic lights change, what should you do ?

Mark one answer
a)   Try to move off before the cyclist.
b)   Allow the cyclist time and room.
c)   Turn right but give the cyclist room.
d)   Tap your horn and drive through first.

Question   16 (5.36)
Why should the junction on the left be kept clear ?

Mark one answer
a)   To allow vehicles to enter and emerge.
b)   To allow the bus to reverse.
c)   To allow vehicles to make a 'U' turn.
d)   To allow vehicles to park.

Question   17 (6.56)
You are driving behind a cyclist. You wish to turn left just ahead. You should

Mark one answer
a)   go around the cyclist on the junction
b)   pull alongside the cyclist and stay level until after the junction
c)   hold back until the cyclist has passed the junction
d)   overtake the cyclist before the junction

Question   18 (6.73)
You are driving behind a moped. You want to turn left just ahead. You should

Mark one answer
a)   overtake the moped before the junction
b)   pull alongside the moped and stay level until just before the junction
c)   sound your horn as a warning and pull in front of the moped
d)   stay behind until the moped has passed the junction.

Question   19 (6.53)
You are following a motorcyclist on an uneven road. You should

Mark one answer
a)   allow less room to ensure that you can be seen in their mirrors
b)   overtake immediately
c)   allow extra room in case they swerve to avoid pot-holes
d)   allow the same room as normal because motorcyclists are not affected by road surfaces.

Question   20 (6.72)
There is a slow-moving motorcyclist ahead of you. You're unsure what the rider is going to do. You should

Mark one answer
a)   pass on the left
b)   pass on the right
c)   stay behind
d)   move closer.

Question   21 (7.18)
You are driving in the right lane of a dual carriageway at 70 mph. You catch up to a lorry which is overtaking another vehicle. You should

Mark one answer
a)   maintain your speed
b)   slow down and keep well back
c)   slow down, but flash your headlamps
d)   maintain your speed and sound your horn

Question   22 (7.2)
It is very windy. You are behind a motorcyclist who is overtaking a high-sided vehicle. What should you do?

Mark one answer
a)   Keep well back
b)   Stay level with the motorcyclist
c)   Keep close to the motorcyclist
d)   Overtake the motorcyclist immediately

Question   23 (2.24)
You are in a line of traffic. The driver behind you is following very closely. What action should you take?

Mark one answer
a)   Slow down, gradually increasing the gap between you and the vehicle in front.
b)   Ignore the following driver and continue to drive within the speed limit.
c)   Signal left and wave the following driver past.
d)   Move out wider to a position just left of the road's centre line.

Question   24 (2.30)
The driver behind is travelling too close to you. You should

Mark one answer
a)   take no action and drive on
b)   slowly accelerate away from the car behind
c)   position your car in the middle of the road
d)   slow down to increase the gap in front

Question   25 (2.32)
A long, heavily loaded lorry is taking a long time to overtake you. What should you do?

Mark one answer
a)   Speed up.
b)   Slow down.
c)   Hold your speed.
d)   Change direction.

85

Question 26 (5.18)
In heavy motorway traffic you are being followed closely by the vehicle behind. How can you lower the risk of an accident?

Mark one answer
a) Increase your distance from the vehicle in front of you
b) Tap your foot on the brake pedal
c) Switch on your hazard lights
d) Move onto the hard shoulder and stop

Question 27 (1.22)
The white arrow means that you should not plan to

Mark one answer
a) slow down
b) turn right
c) overtake
d) turn left

Question 28 (1.33)
To overtake safely, which of the following applies?
.
Mark one answer
a) check the speed and position of following traffic.
b) cut back in sharply when you have passed the vehicle.
c) get in close behind before signalling to move out.
d) steer round the vehicle sharply.

Question 29 (2.34)
You are driving a slow-moving vehicle on a narrow road. When traffic wishes to overtake you should

Mark one answer
a) take no action
b) stop immediately and wave them on
c) pull in safely as soon as you can
d) put your hazard warning lights on

Question 30 (2.33)
You are driving a slow-moving vehicle on a narrow winding road. You should

Mark one answer
a) keep well out to stop vehicles overtaking dangerously
b) wave following vehicles past you if you think they can overtake
c) quickly give a left signal when it is safe for vehicles to overtake you
d) pull in safely when you can to let following vehicles overtake

Question 31 (2.35)
You are driving a slow moving vehicle on a narrow winding road. In order to let other vehicles overtake you should

Mark one answer
a) wave to them to pass
b) pull in when you can do
c) show a left turn signal
d) keep left and hold your speed

Question 32 (4.71)
You should not overtake when

Mark three answers
a) intending to turn left shortly afterwards
b) in a one way street
c) approaching a junction
d) driving up a long hill
e) the view ahead is blocked

Question 33 (8.17)
You wish to overtake on a dual carriageway. You see in your mirror that the car behind has pulled out to overtake you. You should

Mark one answer
a) touch the brakes to show your brake lights
b) signal and pull out to overtake
c) signal to tell the driver behind that you also want to overtake
d) not signal until the car has passed

Question 34 (8.18)
In which THREE of these situations may you overtake another vehicle on the left?

Mark Three answers
a) When the vehicle in front is signalling to turn right
b) When a slower vehicle is travelling in the right-hand lane of a dual carriageway
c) When you are in a one-way street
d) In slow-moving traffic queues when traffic if the right-hand lane is moving more slowly
e) When approaching a motorway slip road where you will be turning off

Question 35 (8.70)
Which TWO are correct? The passing places on a single-track road are

Mark two answers
a) to pull into if the car behind wants to overtake
b) for taking a rest from driving
c) to pull into if an oncoming vehicle wants to proceed
d) to turn the car around, in if you are lost
e) for stopping and checking your route

Question 36 (8.71)
You see a vehicle coming towards you on a single-track road. You should

Mark one answer
a) stop at a passing place
b) put on your hazard flashers
c) reverse back to the main road
d) do an emergency stop

Question 37 (1.23)
This road marking warns

Mark one answer
a) drivers to use the hard shoulder
b) overtaking drivers there is a bend to the left
c) overtaking drivers to move back to the left
d) drivers that it is safe to overtake

Question 38 (1.24)
You are driving along this narrow country road. When passing the cyclist you should drive

Mark one answer
a) slowly sounding the horn as you pass
b) quickly leaving plenty of room
c) slowly leaving plenty of room
d) quickly sounding the horn as you pass

Question 39 (6.55)
You should NEVER attempt to overtake a cyclist

Mark one answer
a) on a one-way street
b) just before you turn right
c) just before you turn left
d) on a dual carriageway

Question 40 (6.60)
When you are overtaking a cyclist you should leave as much room as you would give to a car. Why is this?

Mark one answer
a) The cyclist might change lanes
b) The cyclist might swerve
c) The cyclist might have to make a right turn
d) The cyclist might get off the bike

Question 41 (6.61)
Which TWO should you allow extra room when overtaking?

Mark two answers
a) Tractors
b) Road-sweeping vehicles
c) Motorcycles
d) Bicycles

Question 42 (6.62)
Why should you allow extra room when overtaking a motorcyclist on a windy day?

Mark one answer
a) The rider may be travelling faster than normal
b) The rider may turn off suddenly to get out of the wind
c) The rider may stop suddenly
d) The rider may be blown across in front of you

Question 43 (7.3)
It is very windy. You are about to overtake a motorcyclist. You should

Mark one answer
a) overtake slowly
b) allow extra room
c) sound your horn
d) keep close as you pass.

Question 44 (7.4)
You are about to overtake a slow moving motorcyclist. Which one of these signs would make you take special care ?

Mark one answer

a)   b)

c)   d)

Question 45 (2.59)
When overtaking a horse and rider you should

Mark one answer
a) sound your horn as a warning
b) go past as quickly as possible
c) flash your headlamps as a warning
d) go past slowly and carefully

Question 46 (6.89)
How should you overtake horse riders?

Mark one answer
a) Drive up close and overtake as soon as possible
b) Use your horn just once to warn them
c) Speed is not important but allow plenty of room
d) Drive slowly and leave plenty of room

87

Question 47 (10.17)
There is a tractor ahead of you. You wish to overtake but you are NOT sure if it is safe to do so. You should

Mark one answer
a) follow another overtaking vehicle through
b) sound your horn to the slow vehicle to pull over
c) speed through but flash your lights to oncoming traffic
d) not overtake if you are in doubt.

Question 48 (1.20)
In which of these situations should you avoid overtaking?

Mark one answer
a) Just after a bend
b) In a one-way street
c) On a 30mph road
d) Approaching a dip in the road

Question 49 (7.14)
Before overtaking a large vehicle you should keep well back. Why is this?

Mark one answer
a) To get the best view of the road ahead
b) To give acceleration space to overtake quickly on blind bends
c) To leave a gap in case the vehicle stops and rolls back
d) To offer other drivers a safe gap if they want to overtake you

Question 50 (7.20)
The FIRST thing you should do when you want to overtake a large lorry is

Mark one answer
a) move close behind so you can pass quickly
b) keep in close to the left-hand side
c) stay well back to get a better view
d) flash your headlights and wait for the driver to wave you on

Question 51 (1.19)
You wish to overtake a long, slow-moving vehicle on a busy road. You should

Mark one answer
a) keep well back until you can see it is clear
b) wait behind until the driver waves you past
c) flash your headlights for the oncoming traffic to give way
d) follow it closely and keep moving out to see the road ahead

Question 52 (7.17)
When about to overtake a long vehicle you should

Mark one answer
a) flash your lights and wait for the driver to signal when it is safe
b) drive close to the lorry in order to pass more quickly
c) stay well back from the lorry to obtain a better view
d) sound the horn to warn the driver you are there

Question 53 (7.19)
Why is passing a lorry more risky than passing a car?

Mark one answer
a) The brakes of lorries are not as good
b) Lorries may suddenly pull up
c) Lorries climb hills more slowly
d) Lorries are longer than cars

Question 54 (6.88)
Which THREE should you do when passing sheep on a road?

Mark three answers
a) Allow plenty of room.
b) Drive very slowly.
c) Briefly sound your horn.
d) Be ready to stop.
e) Pass quickly but quietly.

Question 55 (10.16)
You meet an obstruction on your side of the road. You must

Mark one answer
a) wave oncoming vehicles through
b) accelerate to get past first
c) give way to oncoming traffic
d) drive on, it is your right of way

Question 56 (7.32)
Some two way roads are divided into three lanes. Why are these particularly dangerous?

Mark one answer
a) Traffic in both directions can use the middle lane to overtake.
b) Traffic can travel faster in poor weather conditions.
c) Traffic can overtake on the left.
d) Traffic uses the middle lane for emergencies only.

Question 57 (10.35)
On a three-lane dual carriageway the right-hand lane can be used for

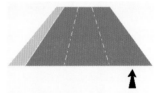

Mark one answer
a) fast-moving traffic
b) turning right only, never overtaking
c) overtaking or turning right
d) overtaking only, never turning right

Question 58 (10.38)
You are driving on a two-lane dual carriageway. For which TWO of these would you use the right-hand lane?

Mark two answers
a) Turning right
b) Normal driving
c) Constant high-speed driving
d) Mending punctures
e) Overtaking slower traffic
f) Driving at the minimum allowed speed

Question 59 (10.49)
Where may you overtake on a one-way street?

Mark one answer
a) Either on the right or the left
b) Only on the left-hand side
c) Only on the right-hand side
d) Overtaking is not allowed

Question 60 (10.50)
You are going along a single-track road with passing places only on the right. The driver behind wishes to overtake. You should

Mark one answer
a) switch on your hazard warning lights
b) wait opposite a passing place on your right
c) speed up to get away from the following driver
d) drive into a passing place on your right

Question 61 (10.51)
You are on a road which is only wide enough for one vehicle. There is a car coming towards you. Which TWO of these would be correct?

Mark two answers
a) Pull into a passing place if your vehicle is wider
b) Wait opposite a passing place on your left
c) Wait opposite a passing place on your right
d) Pull into a passing place on your left
e) Force the other driver to reverse
f) Pull into a passing place on your right

Question 62 (11.111)
The white line painted in the centre of the road means

Mark one answer
a) the area is hazardous and you must not overtake
b) you should give priority to oncoming vehicles
c) do not cross the line unless the road ahead is clear
d) the area is a national speed limit zone

Question 63 (11.114)
You see this white arrow on the road ahead. It means

Mark one answer
a) entrance on the left
b) all vehicles turn left
c) keep left of the hatched markings
d) road bending to the left

Question 64 (11.70)
What does this sign mean?

Mark one answer
a) Two-way traffic ahead across a one-way street
b) Motorway contraflow system ahead
c) Traffic approaching you have priority
d) Two-way traffic straight ahead

Question 65 (11.73)
You are about to overtake when you see this sign. You should

Mark one answer
a) overtake the other driver as quickly as possible
b) move to the right to get a better view
c) switch your headlights on before overtaking
d) hold back until you can see clearly ahead.

89

Question 66 (11.141)

When may you NOT overtake on the left?

Mark one answer

a) On a one-way street
b) When the car in front is signalling to turn right
c) On a free-flowing motorway or dual carriageway
d) When the traffic is moving slowly in queues

Question 67 (11.17)

What does this sign mean?

Mark one answer

a) Two way traffic
b) No right turn ahead
c) Oncoming cars have priority
d) Do not overtake

Question 68 (11.18)

What does this sign mean?

Mark one answer

a) Two way traffic
b) No overtaking
c) You have priority
d) No motor vehicles

Question 69 (11.19)

What does this sign mean?

Mark one answer

a) Keep in one lane
b) Form two lanes
c) Priority to traffic coming toward you
d) Do not overtake

Question 70 (11.20)

Which sign means no overtaking?

Sign A

Sign B

Sign C

Sign D

Mark one answer

a) Sign A
b) Sign B
c) Sign C
d) Sign D

Lesson Introduction

The aim of this lesson is to prepare you for dealing with much busier traffic situations. It will cover the importance of being alert and keeping a reasonable safety gap between you and other vehicles. It will cover some of the problems that arise when you meet oncoming traffic situations where priority may not be obvious. Finally it will also cover level crossings in preparation for practical lesson 10.

This lesson would be undertaken before practical lesson 9 "Roundabouts".

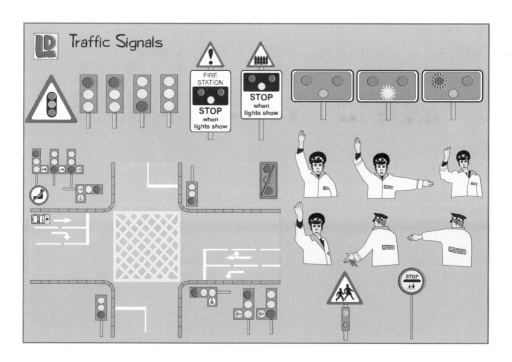

Lesson Study References

Lesson Quiz

Question   1 (1.21)
Which of the following may cause loss of concentration on a long journey?

Mark four answers
a)   Loud music.
b)   Arguing with a passenger.
c)   Using a mobile phone.
d)   Putting in a cassette tape.
e)   Stopping regularly to rest.
f)   Pulling up to tune the radio.

Question   2 (8.89)
Which THREE are likely to make you lose concentration while driving?

Mark three answers
a)   Looking at road maps
b)   Listening to loud music
c)   Using a mobile phone
d)   Using your windscreen washers
e)   Looking in your wing mirror

Question   3 (5.87)
To help concentration on long journeys you should stop frequently and

Mark one answer
a)   have a rest
b)   fill up with fuel
c)   eat a meal
d)   have a drink

Question   4 (5.62)
What else can seriously affect your concentration when driving, other than alcoholic drinks?

Mark three answers
a)   Drugs
b)   Tiredness
c)   Tinted windows
d)   Contact lenses
e)   Loud music

Question   5 (5.95)
Another driver's behaviour has upset you. It may help if you

Mark one answer
a)   stop and take a break
b)   shout abusive language
c)   gesture to them with your hand
d)   follow their car, flashing the headlights.

Question   6 (5.73)
You are not sure if your cough medicine will affect your driving. What TWO things could you do?

Mark two answers
a)   Ask a friend or relative for advice
b)   Check the medicine label
c)   Ask your doctor
d)   Drive if you feel ok

Question   7 (5.74)
You take some cough medicine given to you by a friend. What must you do before driving?

Mark one answer
a)   Check the label to see if the medicine will affect your driving
b)   Ask your friend if taking the medicine affected their driving
c)   Make a short journey to see if the medicine is affecting your driving
d)   Drink some strong coffee

Question   8 (5.69)
Your doctor has given you a course of medicine. Why should you ask if it OK to drive?

Mark one answer
a)   Drugs make you a better driver by quickening your reactions.
b)   You'll have to let your insurance company know about the medicine.
c)   Some types of medicine can cause your reactions to slow down.
d)   The medicine you take may affect your hearing.

Question   9 (5.75)
You have taken medication that may make you feel drowsy. Your friends tell you it is safe to drive. What should you do?

Mark one answer
a)   Take their advice and drive.
b)   Ignore your friends' advice and do not drive.
c)   Only drive if they come with you.
d)   Drive for short distances only.

Question   10 (5.70)
You have been taking medicine for a few days which made you feel drowsy. Today you feel better but still need to take the medicine. You should only drive

Mark one answer
a)   if your journey is necessary
b)   at night on quiet roads
c)   if someone goes with you
d)   after checking with your doctor

Quetion   11 (5.72)
During periods of illness your ability to drive may be impaired. You must

Mark two answers
a)   see your doctor each time before you drive
b)   only take smaller doses of any medicines
c)   be medically fit to drive
d)   not drive after taking certain medicines
e)   take all your medicines with you when you drive.

Question   12 (5.55)
After passing your driving test, you suffer from ill health. This affects your driving. You must

Mark one answer
a)   inform your local police station
b)   get on as best you can
c)   not inform anyone as you hold a full licence
d)   inform the licensing authority

Question 13 (5.76)
You feel drowsy when driving. You should

Mark two answers
a) stop and rest as soon as possible
b) turn the heater up to keep you warm and comfortable
c) make sure you have a good supply of fresh air
d) continue with your journey but drive more slowly
e) close the car windows to help you concentrate

Question 14 (5.80)
If you are feeling tired it is best to stop as soon as you can. Until then you should

Mark one answer
a) ensure a supply of fresh air
b) increase your speed to find a stopping place quickly
c) gently tap the steering wheel
d) keep changing speed to improve concentration

Question 15 (5.81)
Your reactions will be much slower when driving

Mark one answer
a) if tired
b) in fog
c) too quickly
d) in rain.

Question 16 (5.79)
You are about to drive home. You feel very tired and have a severe headache. You should

Mark one answer
a) wait until you are fit and well before driving
b) drive home but take a tablet for headaches
c) drive home if you can stay awake for the journey
d) wait for a short time then drive home slowly

Question 17 (5.86)
Driving long distances can be tiring. You can prevent this by

Mark three answers
a) stopping every so often for a walk
b) opening a window for some fresh air
c) ensuring plenty of refreshment breaks
d) playing loud music on the radio
e) completing the journey without stopping
f) eating a large meal before driving

Question 18 (2.19)
What is meant by 'defensive' driving?

Mark one answer
a) being alert and thinking ahead.
b) Always driving slowly and gently.
c) Always letting others go first.
d) Pulling over for faster traffic.

Question 19 (6.105)
A friend wants to teach you to drive a car. They must

Mark one answer
a) be over 21 and have held a full licence for at least two years
b) be over 18 and hold an advanced driver's certificate
c) be over 18 and have fully comprehensive insurance
d) be over 21 and have held a full licence for at least three years.

Question 20 (2.12)
You could use the 'Two-Second Rule'

Mark one answer
a) before restarting the engine after it's stalled
b) to keep a safe gap from the vehicle in front
c) before using the 'mirror, signal, manoeuvre routine
d) when emerging on wet roads.

Question 21 (2.13)
A two-second gap between yourself and the car in front is sufficient when conditions are

Mark one answer
a) good
b) damp
c) foggy
d) wet

Question 22 (2.9)
In fast traffic a 2 second gap may be enough only when conditions are

Mark one answer
a) dry
b) wet
c) damp
d) foggy

Question 23 (4.14)
You are on a fast, open road in good conditions. For safety, the distance between you and the vehicle in front should be

Mark one answer
a) one car length
b) a two-second time gap
c) 2 metres (6 feet 6 inches)
d) two car lengths

Question 24 (4.15)
The two second rule helps you to

Mark one answer
a) keep a safe distance from the car in front
b) keep the correct distance from the kerb
c) check your blind spot
d) check your mirrors

Question 25 (9.45)

The minimum safe gap to keep between you and the vehicle in front in good conditions is at least

Mark one answer
a) four seconds
b) one second
c) three seconds
d) two seconds

Question 26 (2.20)

You are following a vehicle on a wet road. You should leave a time gap of at least

Mark one answer
a) three seconds
b) one second
c) four seconds
d) two seconds

Question 27 (5.44)

The traffic ahead of you in the left lane is slowing. You should

Mark two answers
a) be wary of cars on your right cutting in
b) accelerate past the vehicles in the left lane
c) pull up on the left hand verge
d) move across and continue in the right hand lane
e) slow down keeping a safe separation distance

Question 28 (8.12)

You are following a vehicle at a safe distance on a wet road. Another driver overtakes you and pulls into the gap you had left. What should you do?

Mark one answer
a) Try to overtake safely as soon as you can
b) Drop back to regain a safe distance
c) Flash your headlights as a warning
d) Stay close to the other vehicle until it moves on

Question 29 (8.15)

You are driving in the left-hand lane of a dual carriageway. Another vehicle overtakes and pulls in front of you leaving you without enough separation distance. You should

Mark one answer
a) continue as you are
b) sound your horn
c) move to the right lane
d) drop back

Question 30 (2.14)

'Tailgating' means

Mark one answer
a) using the rear door of a hatchback car
b) reversing into a parking space
c) following another vehicle too closely
d) driving with rear fog lights on.

Question 31 (7.28)

What does 'tailgating' mean?

Mark one answer
a) When a vehicle delivering goods has its tailgate down.
b) When a vehicle is travelling with its back doors open.
c) When a driver is following another vehicle too closely.
d) When stationary vehicles are too close in a queue.

Question 32 (2.21)

You are driving along this road. The red van cuts in close in front of you. What should you do?

Mark one answer
a) Accelerate to get closer to the red van.
b) Give a long blast on the horn
c) Drop back to leave the correct separation distance
d) Flash your headlights several times.

Question 33 (5.23)

You have just been overtaken by this motorcyclist who is cutting in sharply. You should

Mark one answer
a) sound the horn
b) brake firmly
c) keep a safe gap
d) remember to flash your lights

Question   34 (5.45)
What might you expect to happen in this situation ?

Mark one answer
a)   Traffic will move into the right hand lane.
b)   Traffic speed will increase.
c)   Traffic will move into the left hand lane.
d)   Traffic will not need to change position.

Question   35 (7.13)
You keep well back while waiting to overtake a large vehicle. Another car fills the gap. You should

Mark one answer
a)   sound your horn
b)   drop back further
c)   flash your headlights
d)   start to overtake.

Question   36 (2.57)
You are driving along a country road. A horse and rider are approaching. What should you do?

Mark two answers
a)   Increase your speed.
b)   Sound your horn.
c)   Flash your headlights.
d)   Drive slowly past.
e)   Give plenty of room.
f)   Rev your engine.

Question   37 (6.90)
You notice horse riders in front. What should you do FIRST?

Mark one answer
a)   Be prepared to slow down
b)   Pull out to the middle of the road
c)   Signal right
d)   Accelerate around them

Question   38 (6.91)
As you are driving along you meet a group of horses and riders from a riding school. Why should you be extra cautious?

Mark one answer
a)   They will be moving slowly
b)   They will be moving in single file
c)   Many of the riders may be learners
d)   The horses will panic more because they are in a group

Question   39 (6.92)
You are driving on a narrow country road. Where would you find it most difficult to see horses and riders ahead of you?

Mark one answer
a)   On right-hand bends
b)   When travelling uphill
c)   When travelling downhill
d)   On left-hand bends

Question   40 (6.93)
A horse rider is in the left lane approaching a roundabout. The driver behind should expect the rider to

Mark one answer
a)   turn left
b)   go ahead
c)   go in any direction
d)   turn right

Question   41 (6.95)
You see some horse riders as you approach a roundabout. They are signalling right but keeping well to the left. You should

Mark one answer
a)   proceed as normal
b)   keep close to them
c)   cut in front of them
d)   stay well back

Question   42 (5.94)
Another driver does something that upsets you. You should

Mark one answer
a)   flash your head lamps several times
b)   try not to react
c)   let them know how you feel
d)   sound your horn

Question 43 (1.17)
As you approach this bridge you should

Mark three answers
a) move into the middle of the road to get a better view
b) slow down
c) get over the bridge as quickly as possible
d) consider using your horn
e) find another route
f) beware of pedestrians.

Question 44 (12.34)
To supervise a leaner driver you MUST

Mark two answers
a) hold an advanced driving certificate
b) have held a full licence for at least three years
c) be an approved driving instructor
d) be at least 21

Question 45 (5.33)
What type of vehicle could you expect to meet in the middle of the road ?

Mark one answer
a) Lorry.
b) Bicycle.
c) Car.
d) Motorcycle.

Question 46 (5.32)
When approaching this bridge you should give way to

Mark one answer
a) bicycles
b) buses
c) motorcycles
d) cars

Question 47 (11.65)
What does this sign mean?

Mark one answer
a) Low bridge ahead.
b) Tunnel ahead.
c) Ancient monument ahead.
d) Accident black spot ahead.

Question 48 (11.85)
You are driving through a tunnel and you see this sign. What does it mean ?

Mark one answer
a) Direction to emergency pedestrian exit.
b) Beware of pedestrians, no footpath ahead.
c) No access for pedestrians.
d) Beware of pedestrians crossing ahead.

Question 49 (11.68)
Which of these signs means the end of a dual carriageway?

Mark one answer

Sign A   Sign B

Sign C   Sign D

Question 50 (11.69)
What does this sign mean?

Mark one answer
a) End of dual carriageway.
b) Tall bridge.
c) Road narrows.
d) End of narrow bridge.

Question 51 (6.108)
You are dazzled at night by a vehicle behind you. You should

Mark one answer
a) set your mirror to anti dazzle
b) set your mirror to dazzle the other driver
c) brake sharply to a stop
d) switch your rear lights on and off

Question 52 (7.16)
You are driving downhill. There is a car parked on the other side of the road. Large, slow lorries are coming towards you. You should

Mark one answer
a) keep going because you have the right of way
b) slow down and give way
c) speed up and get past quickly
d) pull over on the right behind the parked car.

Question 53 (11.29)
What does this traffic sign mean?

Mark one answer
a) One-way traffic only
b) No overtaking allowed
c) No U-turns
d) Give priority to oncoming traffic

Question 54 (11.30)
What is the meaning of this traffic sign?

Mark one answer
a) Give priority to vehicles coming toward you
b) Bus lane ahead
c) You have priority over vehicles coming toward you
d) End of two-way

Question 55 (11.31)
Which sign means 'traffic has priority over oncoming vehicles'?

Mark one answer

Sign A

Sign B

Sign C

Sign D

Question 56 (11.33)
What does this sign mean?

Mark one answer
a) Two-way traffic ahead
b) You have priority over vehicles from the opposite direction
c) You are entering a one-way street
d) No overtaking

Question 57 (4.54)
In very hot weather the road surface can get soft. Which TWO of the following will be affected most?

Mark two answers
a) The steering.
b) The braking.
c) The suspension.
d) The windscreen.

Question 58 (8.67)
When driving towards a bright setting sun, glare can be reduced by

Mark one answer
a) closing one eye
b) dipping the interior mirror
c) wearing dark glasses
d) looking sideways.

Question 59 (5.12)
What should the driver of a car coming up to this level crossing do?

Mark one answer
a) Switch on hazard warning lights
b) Drive through carefully
c) Drive through quickly
d) Stop before the barrier

Question 60 (5.28)
You are driving towards this level crossing. What would be the first warning of an approaching train ?

Mark one answer
a) Both half barriers down.
b) A steady amber light.
c) One half barrier down.
d) Twin flashing red lights.

Question 61 (5.34)
As the driver of this vehicle, why should you slow down ?

Mark two answers
a) Because of the bend.
b) Because its hard to see to the right.
c) Because of approaching trains.
d) Because of animals crossing.
e) Because of the level crossing.

Question 62 (10.73)
You are waiting at a level crossing. The red warning lights continues to flash after a train has passed by. What should you do?

Mark one answer
a) Drive across carefully
b) Continue to wait
c) Get out and investigate
d) Telephone the signal operator

Question 63 (10.74)
You are driving over a level crossing. The warning lights come on and a bell rings. What should you do?

Mark one answer
a) Stop immediately and use your hazard warning lights
b) Stop and reverse back to clear the crossing
c) Keep going and clear the crossing
d) Get everyone out of the vehicle immediately

Question 64 (10.76)
You will see these markers when approaching

Mark one answer
a) a concealed level crossing
b) the end of a motorway
c) a concealed 'road narrows' sign
d) the end of a dual carriageway.

Question 65 (10.75)
You are waiting at a level crossing. A train has passed but the lights keep flashing. You must

Mark one answer
a) park your vehicle and investigate
b) edge over the stop line and look for trains
c) carry on waiting
d) phone the signal operator

Question 66 (11.74)
What does this sign mean ?

Mark one answer
a) Level crossing with gate or barrier.
b) Gated road ahead.
c) Level crossing without gate or barrier.
d) Cattle grid ahead.

Question 67 (13.55)
At a railway level crossing the red light signal continues to flash after a train has gone by. What should you do?

Mark one answer
a) Proceed with caution
b) Alert drivers behind you
c) Wait
d) Phone the signal operator

Question 68 (13.56)
You break down on a level crossing. The lights have not yet begun to flash. Which THREE things should you do?

Mark three answers
a) Telephone the signal operator
b) Leave your vehicle and get everyone clear
c) Walk down the track and signal the next train
d) Move the vehicle if a signal operator tells you to
e) Tell drivers behind what has happened

Question 69 (13.57)
You have stalled in the middle of a level crossing and cannot restart the engine. The warning bell starts to ring. You should

Mark one answer
a) get out and clear of the crossing
b) push the vehicle clear of the crossing
c) carry on trying to restart the engine
d) run down the track to warn the signalman

Question   70 (13.58)
Your vehicle has broken down on an
automatic railway level crossing. What
should you do FIRST?

Mark one answer

a)   Get everyone out of the vehicle
     and clear of the crossing
b)   Walk along the track to give
     warning to any approaching trains
c)   Phone the signal operator so that
     trains can be stopped
d)   Try to push the vehicle clear of
     the crossing as soon as possible

Lesson Introduction

Once you have become familiar with dealing with busier traffic
situations you will start to move into areas where you are likely to
come across more and more pedestrians i.e. busy shopping areas,
town and city centres. During this lesson you will cover all the theory test
questions that relate to pedestrians and the types of crossings they use.

This lesson would be undertaken before practical lesson 10 "Traffic signals
and pedestrian crossings".

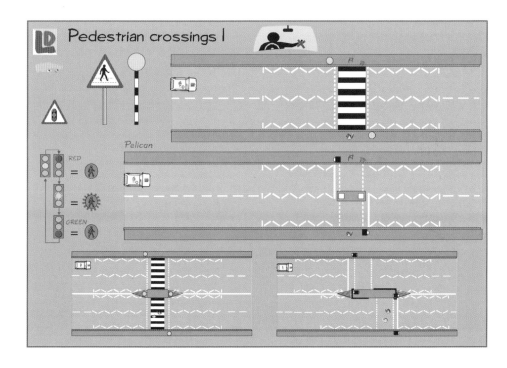

Lesson Study References

Lesson Quiz

Question 1 (2.22)
While driving you approach a large puddle thats close to the left-hand kerb. Pedestrians are close to the water. You should

Mark two answer
a) ignor the puddle
b) brake suddenly and sound your horn
c) slow down before the puddle
d) try to avoid splashing the pedestrians
e) wave at the pedestrians to keep back

Question 2 (5.8)
What should the driver of the red (arrowed) car do?

Mark one answer
a) Wave the pedestrians who are waiting to cross
b) Wait for the pedestrian in the road to cross
c) Quickly drive behind the pedestrian in the road
d) Tell the pedestrian in the road she should not have crossed

Question 3 (6.4)
You are driving on a country road. What should you expect to see coming towards you on YOUR side of the road

Mark one answer
a) Pedestrians.
b) Horse riders.
c) Motorcycles.
d) Bicycles.

Question 4 (5.31)
You are driving towards this left hand bend. What dangers should you be aware of ?

Mark one answer
a) A vehicle overtaking you.
b) No white lines in the centre of the road.
c) No sign to warn you of the bend.
d) Pedestrians walking towards you.

Question 5 (2.56)
You wish to turn right ahead. Why should you take up the correct position in good time?

Mark one answer
a) To allow other drivers to pull out in front of you.
b) To give a better view into the road that you're joining.
c) To help other road users know what you intend to do.
d) To allow drivers to pass you on the right.

Question 6 (5.25)
What is the main hazard in this picture

Mark one answer
a) The pedestrian.
b) The parked cars.
c) The junction on the left.
d) The driveway on the left.

Question 7 (6.5)
Which sign means there may be people walking along the road?

Sign A   Sign B

Sign C   Sign D

Mark one answer
a) Sign A
b) Sign B
c) Sign C
d) Sign D

Question 8 (6.7)
You are turning left into a side road. Pedestrians are crossing the road near the junction . You must

Mark one answer
a) wait for them to cross
b) wave them on
c) sound your horn
d) switch on your hazard lights

Question 9 (6.8)
You are turning left at a junction. Pedestrians have started to cross the road. You should

Mark one answer
a) go on, giving plenty of room
b) stop and wave at them to cross
c) give way to them
d) blow your horn and proceed

Question 10 (6.9)
You are turning left from a main road into a side road. People are already crossing the road into which you are turning. You should

Mark one answer
a) wait and allow them to cross
b) continue, as it is your right of way
c) signal to them to continue crossing
d) sound your horn to warn them of your presence

Question 11 (6.10)
You are at a road junction, turning into a minor road. There are pedestrians crossing the minor road. You should

Mark one answer
a) stop and wave the pedestrians across
b) carry on, the pedestrians should give way to you
c) give way to the pedestrians who are already crossing
d) sound your horn to let the pedestrians know you are there

Question 12 (6.86)
You are driving in town. There is a bus at the bus stop on the other side of the road. Why should you be careful?

Mark one answer
a) The bus may have broken down
b) Pedestrians may come from behind the bus
c) The bus may remain stationary
d) The bus may move of suddenly

Question 13 (6.106)
Your vehicle hits a pedestrian at 40 mph. The pedestrian

Mark one answer
a) will probably survive
b) will probably be killed
c) will certainly survive
d) will certainly be killed

Question 14 (6.6)
What does this sign mean?

Mark one answer
a) Pedestrian crossing.
b) Pedestrians in the road ahead.
c) No pedestrians.
d) Route for pedestrians.

Question 15 (6.107)
At night you see a pedestrian wearing reflective clothing and carrying a bright red light. What does this mean?

Mark one answer
a) You are approaching roadworks.
b) You are approaching an organised march.
c) You are approaching a slow-moving vehicle.
d) You are approaching an accident black spot.

Question 16 (6.109)
A pedestrian steps out into the road just ahead of you. What should you do FIRST?

Mark one answer
a) Sound your horn.
b) Check your mirror.
c) Flash your headlights.
d) Press the brake.

Question   17 (6.43)
Which sign tells you that pedestrians may be walking in the road as there is no pavement?

Mark one answer

Sign A

Sign B

Sign C   Sign D

Question   18 (6.44)
Which sign means there may be elderly pedestrians likely to cross the road ?

Mark one answer

Sign A

Sign B

Sign C   Sign D

Question   19 (6.50)
You see two elderly pedestrians about to cross the road ahead. You should

Mark one answer
a)   expect them to wait for you to pass
b)   speed up to get past them quickly
c)   stop and wave them across the road
d)   be careful, they may misjudge your speed

Question   20 (11.58)
Which sign means that pedestrians may be walking along the road?

Mark one answer

Sign A   Sign B

Sign C   Sign D

Question   21 (6.49)
What action would you take when elderly people are crossing the road?

Elderly people

Mark one answer
a)   Wave them across so they know that you've seen them.
b)   Be patient and allow them to cross in their own time.
c)   Rev the engine to let them know that you're waiting.
d)   Tap the horn in case they are hard of hearing.

Question   22 (6.46)
You see a pedestrian carrying a white stick. This shows that the person is

Mark one answer
a)   elderly
b)   deaf
c)   blind
d)   disabled

Question   23 (6.47)
You see a pedestrian with a white slick and two red reflective bands This means the person is

Mark one answer
a)   deaf and blind
b)   physically disabled
c)   deaf only
d)   blind only

Question   24 (6.32)
What does this sign warn you to look for?

Mark one answer
a)   A pedestrian crossing
b)   School children
c)   A school crossing patrol
d)   A park

Question   25 (6.28)
Look at this picture. What is the danger you should be most aware of?

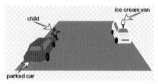

Mark one answer
a)   The car on the left may move off
b)   The child may run out into the road
c)   The ice cream van may move off
d)   The driver of the ice cream van may get out

105

Question 26 (6.30)
You are driving past a line of parked cars. You notice a ball bouncing out into the road ahead. What should you do?

Mark one answer
a) Continue driving at the same speed and sound your horn
b) Slow down and be prepared to stop for children
c) Continue driving at the same speed and flash your headlights
d) Stop and wave the children across to fetch their ball

Question 27 (6.102)
Which age group is most likely to be involved in a road accident?

Mark one answer
a) 55 year-olds and over
b) 46 to 55 year-olds
c) 17 to 25 year-olds
d) 36 to 45 year-olds

Question 28 (2.23)
When driving in towns you should always

Mark one answer
a) stay well away from the kerb in busy shopping streets
b) remain stopped at a flashing amber light at pelican crossings
c) weave in and out when passing parked vehicles
d) wave pedestrians across at zebra crossings

Question 29 (2.63)
When should you beckon pedestrians to cross the road?

Mark one answer
a) At pedestrian crossings.
b) At no time.
c) At junctions.
d) At school crossings.

Question 30 (10.22)
You are finding it difficult to find a parking place in busy town. You can see there is space on the zig zag lines of a zebra crossing. Can you park there ?

Mark one answer
a) No, unless you stay with your car.
b) Yes, in order to drop off a passenger.
c) Yes, if you do not block peope from crossing.
d) No, not in any circumstances.

Question 31 (11.108)
What do these zigzag lines at pedestrian crossings mean?

Mark one answer
a) Parking allowed only for a short time
b) No parking at any time
c) Slow down to 20 mph
d) Sounding horns is not allowed

Question 32 (2.61)
You are waiting at a crossing controlled by a policeman. A pedestrian is crossing. You are signalled to move on. You should

Mark one answer
a) drive on immediately.
b) sound your horn
c) rev your engine and begin to move forward.
d) wait until the pedestrian has crossed.

Question 33 (2.5)
You have stopped at a pedestrian crossing. To allow pedestrians to cross you should

Mark one answer
a) wait until they have crossed
b) edge your vehicle forward slowly
c) wait, revving your engine
d) signal to pedestrians to cross.

Question 34 (6.27)
When may you stop on a pedestrian crossing?

Mark one answer
a) When there is a queue of traffic in front of you
b) To avoid an accident
c) Not at any time
d) Between the hours of 11 pm and 7 am

Question 35 (11.60)
What does this sign mean?

Mark one answer
a) No footpath ahead
b) Pedestrians only ahead
c) School ahead
d) Pedestrian crossing ahead

Question 36 (11.61)
What does this sign mean?

Mark one answer
a) Pedestrian crossing ahead
b) Pedestrian zone - no vehicles
c) No pedestrians allowed
d) School crossing patrol

Question 37 (5.26)
You are driving towards this parked lorry. What is the first hazard you should be aware of ?

Mark one answer
a) The lorry moving off.
b) The narrowing road.
c) The pedestrian crossing.
d) The vehicles ahead.

Question 38 (6.48)
You are driving towards a pedestrian crossing. Waiting to cross is a person in a wheelchair. You should

Mark one answer
a) be prepared to stop
b) wave to the person to cross
c) wave to the person to wait
d) continue on your way

Question 39 (11.59)
Whitch of these signs warn you of a pedestrian crossing?

Mark one answer

Sign A   Sign B

Sign C   Sign D

Question 40 (2.4)
You are driving towards a zebra crossing. Pedestrians are waiting to cross. You should

Mark one answer
a) use your headlamps to indicate they can cross
b) slow down and prepare to stop
c) give way to the elderly and infirm only
d) wave at them to cross the road

Question 41 (2.62)
You stop for pedestrians waiting to cross at a Zebra crossing. They do not start to cross. What should you do?

Mark one answer
a) Be patient and wait
b) Drive on
c) Sound your horn
d) Wave them to cross

Question 42 (2.8)
At zebra crossings you should

Mark one answer
a) rev your engine to encourage pedestrians to cross quickly
b) park only on the zig zag lines on the left
c) always leave it clear in traffic queues
d) wave pedestrians to cross if you intend to wait for them

Question 43 (2.7)
Why should you give an arm signal on approach to a zebra crossing?

Mark three answers
a) to warn following traffic.
b) to let pedestrians know you are not stopping.
c) to let pedestrians know you are slowing down.
d) to warn oncoming traffic.
e) to warn traffic you intend to turn.

Question 44 (5.7)
What should the driver of the car approaching the crossing do?

Mark one answer
a) Sound your horn
b) Continue at the same speed
c) Slow and get ready to stop
d) Drive through quickly

Question 45 (10.77)
Someone is waiting to cross at a zebra crossing. They are standing on the pavement. You should normally

Mark one answer
a) go on quickly before they step onto the crossing
b) stop before you reach the zig zag lines and let them cross
c) stop, let them cross, wait patiently
d) ignore them as they are still on the pavement

Question 46 (11.109)
You are approaching a zebra crossing where pedestrians are waiting. Which arm signal might you give?

Mark one answer

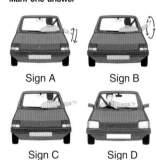

Sign A   Sign B

Sign C   Sign D

Question 47 (2.66)
You should never wave people across at pedestrian crossings because

Mark two answers
a) there may be another vehicle coming
b) they may not be looking
c) it is safer for you to carry on
d) they may not be ready to cross

Question 48 (2.1)
A pelican crossing that crosses the road in a STRAIGHT line and has a central island MUST be treated as

Mark one answer
a) one crossing in daylight only
b) one complete crossing
c) two separate crossings
d) two crossings during darkness.

Question 49 (2.2)
At a pelican crossing the flashing amber light means you should

Mark one answer
a) give way to pedestrians already on the crossing
b) give way to pedestrians waiting to cross
c) stop and wait for the green light
d) stop, if you can do so safely

Question 50 (2.3)
You are approaching a pelican crossing. The amber light is flashing. You must

Mark one answer
a) stop even if the crossing is clear
b) encourage pedestrians to cross
c) not move until the green light appears
d) give way to pedestrians who are crossing

Question 51 (2.67)
Puffin crossings are for use by

Mark one answer
a) cyclists only
b) pedestrians and cyclists
c) horse riders
d) pedestrians only

Question 52 (6.22)
What must a driver do at a pelican crossing when the amber light is flashing?

Mark one answer
a) Signal the pedestrian to cross.
b) Always wait for the green light before proceeding.
c) Give way to any pedestrians on the crossing.
d) Wait for the red–and–amber light before proceeding.

Question 53 (6.52)
As you approach a pelican crossing the lights change to green. Elderly people are halfway across. You should

Mark one answer
a) wave them to cross as quickly as they can
b) rev your engine to make them hurry
c) flash your lights in case they have not heard you
d) wait because they will take longer to cross

Question 54 (10.81)
You are waiting at a pelican crossing. The red light changes to flashing amber. This means you must

Mark one answer
a) wait for pedestrians on the crossing to clear
b) move off immediately without any hesitation
c) wait for the green light before moving off
d) get ready and go when the continuous amber light shows

Question 55 (10.80)
At a pelican crossing what does a flashing amber light mean?

Mark one answer
a) You must give way to pedestrians still on the crossing
b) You must not move off until the lights stop flashing
c) You can move off, even if pedestrians are still on the crossing
d) You must stop because the lights are about to change to red

Question 56 (2.60)
At a puffin crossing what colour follows the green signal?

Mark one answer
a) Steady red.
b) Flashing amber.
c) Steady amber.
d) Flashing green.

Question 57 (2.10)
At puffin crossings which light will not show to a driver?

Mark one answer
a) flashing amber.
b) red.
c) steady amber.
d) green.

Question   58 (2.11)
You are approaching a red light at a puffin crossing. Pedestrians are on the crossing. The red light will stay on until

Mark one answer
a)   you start to edge forward on to the crossing
b)   the pedestrians have reached a safe position
c)   the pedestrians are clear of the front of your vehicle
d)   a driver from the opposite direction reaches the crossing

Question   59 (6.25)
At toucan crossings

Mark two answers
a)   there is no flashing amber light
b)   cyclists are not permitted
c)   there is a continuously flashing amber beacon
d)   pedestrians and cyclists may cross
e)   you only stop if someone is waiting to cross.

Question   60 (6.26)
What type of crossing is this?

Mark one answer
a)   A zebra crossing.
b)   A pelican crossing.
c)   A puffin crossing.
d)   A toucan crossing.

Question   61 (6.24)
A toucan crossing is different from other crossings because

Mark one answer
a)   moped riders can use it
b)   it is controlled by a traffic warden
c)   it is controlled by two flashing lights
d)   cyclists can use it

Question   62 (10.78)
At toucan crossings, apart from pedestrians you should be aware of

Mark one answer
a)   emergency vehicles emerging
b)   buses pulling out
c)   trams crossing in front
d)   cyclists riding across.

Question   63 (10.79)
Who can use a toucan crossing?

Mark two answers
a)   Trains.
b)   Cyclists.
c)   Buses.
d)   Pedestrians.
e)   Trams.

Question   64 (6.33)
How will a school crossing patrol signal you to stop?

Mark one answer
a)   By displaying a stop sign
b)   By giving you an arm signal
c)   By displaying a red light
d)   By pointing to children on the opposite pavement

Question   65 (6.35)
You see someone step onto the road holding this sign. What must you do?

Mark one answer
a)   Pull up before the person
b)   Drive carefully round the person
c)   Slow down and look out for children
d)   Signal the person to cross

Question   66 (6.37)
A school crossing patrol shows a stop children sign. What must you do?

Mark one answer
a)   Stop at all times
b)   Continue if safe to do so
c)   Slow down and be ready to stop
d)   Stop ONLY if children are crossing

Question   67 (6.36)
You are approaching a school crossing patrol. When this sign is held up you must

Mark one answer
a)   Stop and allow any children to cross
b)   Stop only if the children are on a pedestrian crossing
c)   Stop only when the children are actually crossing the road
d)   Stop and beckon the children to cross

Question   68 (6.34)
What warning may you see before a
school 'lollipop warden ?

Mark one answer
a)   One flashing amber light.
b)   Two flashing amber lights.
c)   Two flashing red lights.
d)   One flashing red light.

Question   69 (5.83)
How often should you stop on a long
journey?

Mark one answer
a)   At least every four hours
b)   When you need to eat
c)   When you need petrol
d)   At least every two hours

Question   70 (5.85)
You are planning a long journey. It
should take about six hours. Do
you need to plan rest stops ?

Mark one answer
a)   Yes, you should plan to stop after
     about four hours driving.
b)   Yes, regular stops help
     concentration.
c)   No, you will be less tired if you get
     there as soon as possible.
d)   No, only fuel stops will be needed.

Lesson Introduction

During in this lesson you will be covering the road and weather conditions that can make driving much more hazardous. It also includes the use of the horn the effects of driving at night and some unusual road features such as fords.

This lesson would be undertaken before practical lesson 11 " Defensive driving and perception".

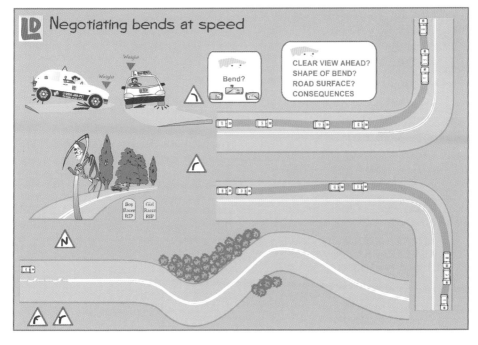

Lesson Study References

Lesson Quiz

Question 1 (2.51)
What should you use your horn for?

Mark one answer
a)   To greet other road users.
b)   To alert others to your presence.
c)   To allow you right of way.
d)   To signal your annoyance.

Question 2 (3.66)
You must NOT sound your horn

Mark one answer
a)   between 11.30 pm and 7 am in a built-up area
b)   at any time in a built-up area
c)   between 10 pm and 6 am in a built-up area
d)   between 11.30 pm and 6 am on any road

Question 3 (3.67)
When should you NOT use your horn in a built-up area?

Mark one answer
a)   Between 9 pm and dawn
b)   Between dusk and 8 am
c)   Between 11.30 pm and 7 am
d)   Between 8 pm and 8 am

Question 4 (11.134)
When may you sound the horn on your vehicle?

Mark one answer
a)   To warn other drivers of your presence
b)   To attract a friend's attention
c)   To make slower drivers move over
d)   To give you right of way

Question 5 (11.135)
You must not use your horn when your vehicle is stationary

Mark one answer
a)   unless a moving vehicle may cause you danger
b)   at any time whatsoever
c)   unless it is used only briefly
d)   except for signalling that you have just arrived

Question 6 (1.29)
You are driving at night and are dazzled by the headlights of an oncoming car. You should

Mark one answer
a)   slow down or stop
b)   close your eyes
c)   pull down the sun visor
d)   flash your headlights

Question 7 (8.64)
You are travelling at night. You are dazzled by headlights coming towards you . You should

Mark one answer
a)   switch on your main beam headlights
b)   put your hand over your eyes
c)   slow down or stop
d)   pull down your sun visor

Question 8 (8.65)
You are dazzled by oncoming headlights when driving at night. What should you do?

Mark one answer
a)   Flash your lights
b)   Slow down or stop
c)   Brake hard
d)   Drive faster past the oncoming car

Question 9 (2.26)
You are waiting in a traffic queue at night. To avoid dazzling following drivers you should

Mark one answer
a)   apply the handbrake only
b)   apply the footbrake only
c)   switch off your headlights
d)   use both the handbrake and footbrake

Question 10 (1.31)
You are driving at dusk. You should switch your lights on

Mark two answers
a)   even when street lights are not lit
b)   so others can see you
c)   only when others have done so
d)   only when street lights are lit

Question 11 (2.15)
You are driving on a clear night. There is a steady stream of oncoming traffic. The national speed limit applies. Which lights should you use?

Mark one answer
a)   Full beam headlights.
b)   Sidelights.
c)   Dipped headlights.
d)   Fog lights.

Question 12 (3.36)
When must you use dipped headlights during the day ?

Mark one answer
a)   All the time.
b)   Along narrow streets.
c)   In poor visibility.
d)   When parking.

Question 13 (11.139)
When may you use hazard warning lights when driving?

Mark one answer
a) Instead of sounding the horn in a built-up area between 11.30pm and 7am.
b) On a motorway or unrestricted dual carriageway, to warn of a hazard ahead.
c) On rural routes, after a warning sign of animals.
d) On the approach to toucan crossing where cyclists are waiting to cross.

Question 14 (8.60)
Which TWO of the following are correct? When overtaking at night you should

Mark two answers
a) beware of bends in the road ahead
b) put headlights on full beam
c) be careful because you can see less
d) sound your horn twice before moving out
e) wait until a bend so you can see the oncoming headlights

Question 15 (8.61)
You are overtaking a car at night. You must be sure that

Mark one answer
a) you have switched your lights to full beam before overtaking
b) your rear fog lights are switched on
c) you flash your head lamps before overtaking
d) you do not dazzle other road users

Question 16 (8.62)
You are driving at night. Why should you be extra careful of your speed?

Mark one answer
a) Because you might need to stop within the distance that you can see.
b) Because it uses more petrol.
c) Because driving with the lights on runs down the battery.
d) Because you may be late.

Question 17 (8.68)
You are on a narrow road at night. A slower-moving vehicle ahead has been signalling right for some time. What should you do?

Mark one answer
a) Flash your headlights before overtaking
b) Signal right and sound your horn
c) Overtake on the left
d) Wait for the signal to be cancelled before overtaking

Question 18 (8.57)
You are driving on a well-lit motorway at night. You must

Mark one answer
a) use headlights only in bad weather
b) always use rear fog lights
c) use only your sidelights
d) always use your headlights

Question 19 (8.58)
You are driving on a motorway at night You MUST have your headlights switched on unless

Mark one answer
a) there are vehicles close in front of you
b) you are travelling below 50 mph
c) your vehicle is broken down on the hard shoulder
d) the motorway is lit

Question 20 (8..59)
You are travelling on a motorway at night with other vehicles just ahead of you. Which lights should you have on?

Mark one answer
a) Dipped headlights
b) Main beam headlights
c) Sidelights only
d) Front fog lights

Question 21 (8.56)
Should lights be used when traveling at night on a well lit motorway ?

Mark one answer
a) Yes, but only side lights are needed.
b) Yes dipped headlights are needed
c) No, unless the weather is bad.
d) No, lights are not needed.

Question 22 (10.36)
You are driving at night with full beam headlights on. A vehicle is overtaking you. You should dip your lights

Mark one answer
a) some time after the vehicle has passed you
b) before the vehicle starts to pass you
c) only if the other driver dips his headlights
d) as soon as the vehicle passes you.

Question 23 (4.24)
You are driving in heavy rain when your steering suddenly becomes very light. To get control again you must

Mark one answer
a) ease of the accelerator
b) brake lightly to reduce speed
c) change down to a lower gear
d) steer towards a dry part of the road

Question 24 (4.25)
You are driving in heavy rain. Your steering suddenly becomes very light. You should

Mark one answer
a) steer towards the side of the road
b) apply gentle acceleration
c) brake firmly to reduce speed
d) ease off the accelerator.

Question 25 (8.19)
You are travellingin very heavy rain. Your overall stopping distance is likely to be

Mark one answer
a) doubled
b) halved
c) up to 10 times greater
d) no different

Question 26 (5.29)
You are driving along this motorway. It is raining. When following this lorry you should

Mark two answers
a) allow at least a two second gap
b) move left and drive on the hard shoulder
c) allow at least a four second gap
d) be aware of spray reducing your vision
e) move right nd stay in the right hand lane

Question 27 (7.30)
You are driving on a wet motorway with surface spray. You should

Mark one answer
a) use dipped headlights
b) drive in any lane with no traffic
c) use your hazard flashers
d) use your rear fog lights

Question 28 (7.31)
You are driving in heavy traffic on a wet road. Spray makes it difficult to be seen. You should use your

Mark two answers
a) full headlights
b) rear fog lights if visibility is less than 100 metres (328 ft)
c) rear fog lights if visibility is more than 100 metres (328 ft)
d) dipped headlights
e) side lights only

Question 29 (8.21)
Give two reasons for using an additive in the windscreen washer reservoir.

Mark two answers
a) To prevent freezing in winter.
b) To wipe off leaves in autumn.
c) To help prevent mould growth.
d) To clear dead insects in summer.
e) To prevent corrosion.

Question 30 (8.35)
You are driving in very wet weather. Your vehicle begins to slide. This effect is called

Mark one answer
a) hosing
b) weaving
c) aquaplaning
d) fading.

Question 31 (4.27)
You have driven through a flood. What is the first thing you should do?

Mark one answer
a) Test your brakes
b) Switch on your windscreen wipers
c) Stop and check the tyres
d) Stop and dry the brakes

Question 32 (4.28)
You are driving along a country road. You see this sign. AFTER dealing safely with the hazard you should always

Mark one answer
a) check your tyre pressures
b) switch on your hazard warning lights
c) switch on your rear fog lamps
d) test your brakes.

Question 33 (8.36)
Why should you test your brakes after this hazard?

Mark one answer
a) Because your brakes will be soaking wet
b) Because you will have driven down a long hill
c) Because you will be driving on a slippery road
d) Because you will have just crossed a long bridge

Question 34 (8.74)
Which of the following may apply when dealing with this hazard?

Mark four answers
a) It could be more difficult in winter
b) Use a low gear and drive slowly
c) Use a high gear to prevent wheelspin
d) Test your brakes afterwards
e) Always switch on fog lamps
f) There may be a depth gauge

Question 35 (11.78)
What does this sign mean?

Mark one answer
a) Uneven road surface.
b) Bridge over the road.
c) Road ahead ends.
d) Water across the road.

Question 36 (4.50)
When driving in fog in daylight you should use

Mark one answer
a) hazard lights
b) dipped headlights
c) full beam headlights
d) sidelights

Question 37 (4.12)
When driving in fog, which of the following are correct ?

Mark three answers
a) Use dipped headlights.
b) Use headlamps on full beam.
c) Allow more time for your journey.
d) Keep close to the car in front.
e) Slow down.
f) Use side lights only.

Question 38 (8.37)
You have to make a journey in fog. What are the TWO most important things you should do before you set out?

Mark two answers
a) Check that your lights are working
b) Top up the radiator with anti-freeze
c) Make sure that the windows are clean
d) Check the battery
e) Make sure you have a warning Triangle in the vehicle

Question 39 (8.40)
You have to make a journey in foggy conditions. You should

Mark one answer
a) leave plenty of time for your journey
b) keep two seconds behind other vehicles
c) follow closely other vehicles tail lights
d) never use de-misters and windscreen wipers

Question 40 (8.42)
You are following other vehicles in fog with your lights on. How else can you reduce the chances of being involved in an accident?

Mark one answer
a) Keep close to the vehicle in front
b) Reduce your speed and increase the gap
c) Use your main beam instead of dipped headlights
d) Keep together with the faster vehicles

Question 41 (8.43)
Why should you always reduce your speed when driving in fog?

Mark one answer
a) Because the engine is colder
b) Because the brakes do not work as well
c) Because it is more difficult to see events ahead
d) Because you could be dazzled by other people's fog lights

Question 42 (8.44)
You are driving in fog. The car behind seems to be very close. You should

Mark one answer
a) switch on your hazard warning lights
b) continue cautiously
c) pull over and stop immediately
d) speed up to get away

Question 43 (8.45)
You are driving in fog. Why should you keep well back from the vehicle in front?

Mark one answer
a) In case it changes direction suddenly
b) In case its brake lights dazzle you
c) In case it stops suddenly
d) In case its fog lights dazzle you

Question 44 (8.46)
You should switch your rear fog lights on when visibility drops below

Mark one answer
a) your overall stopping distance
b) 10 metres (33 feet)
c) 100 metres (330 feet)
d) ten car lengths

Question 45 (8.47)
You are driving in poor visibility. You can see more than 100 metres (330 feet) ahead. How can you make sure other drivers can see you?

Mark one answer
a) Keep well out towards the middle of the road
b) Turn on your dipped headlights
c) Follow the vehicle in front closely
d) Turn on your rear fog lights

Question 46 (8.48)
You should only use rear fog lights when you cannot see further than about

Mark one answer
a) 150 metres (495 feet)
b) 100 metres (330 feet)
c) 200 metres (660 feet)
d) 250 metres (800 feet)

Question 47 (8.50)
You have to park on the road in fog. You should

Mark one answer
a) leave dipped headlights and fog lights on
b) leave sidelights on
c) leave dipped headlights on
d) leave main beam headlights on

Question 48 (8.53)
You are driving on a motorway in fog. The left-hand edge of the motorway can be identified by reflective studs. What colour are they?

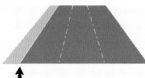

Mark one answer
a) Red
b) Green
c) White
d) Amber

Question 49 (8.49)
Whilst driving, the fog clears and you can see more clearly. You must remember to

Mark one answer
a) switch off the fog lights
b) reduce your speed
c) switch off the demister
d) close any open windows.

Question 50 (8.51)
On a foggy day you unavoidably have to park your car on the road. You should

Mark one answer
a) leave your headlights on
b) leave your fog lights on
c) leave your sidelights on
d) leave your hazard lights on.

Question 51 (8.41)
When travelling home the weather becomes foggy. Your daytime visibility is reduced to 80 metres (262 ft). You should

Mark one answer
a) switch on side lights only
b) switch on hazard warning lights
c) leave lights switched off unless conditions worsen
d) switch on dipped headlights and rear fog lamps

Question 52 (4.47)
You are trying to move off on snow. You should use

Mark one answer
a) the lowest gear you can
b) the highest gear you can
c) a high engine speed
d) the handbrake and footbrake together

Question 53 (4.48)
When driving in falling snow you should

Mark one answer
a) brake firmly and quickly
b) be ready to steer sharply
c) use sidelights only
d) brake gently in plenty of time

Question 54 (4.45)
You are driving in falling snow. Your wipers are not clearing the windscreen. You should

Mark one answer
a) set the windscreen demister to cool
b) be prepared to clear the windscreen by hand
c) use the windscreen washers
d) partly open the front windows

Question 55 (4.44)
Before starting a journey in freezing weather you should clear ice and snow from your vehicle

Mark four answers
a) aerial
b) windows
c) bumper
d) lights
e) mirrors
f) number plates

Question 56 (4.46)
When driving in snow it is best to keep in as high a gear as possible. Why is this?

Mark one answer
a) So that wheelspin does not cause your engine to run too fast
b) To help to prevent wheelspin
c) To help you slow down quickly when you brake
d) To leave a lower gear available in case of wheelspin

Question 57 (8.32)
How can you best control your vehicle when driving in snow?

Mark one answer
a) By driving in first gear
b) By driving slowly in as high a gear as possible
c) By staying in low gear and gripping the steering wheel tightly
d) By keeping the engine revs high and slipping the clutch

Question 58 (8.31)
When snow is falling heavily you should

Mark one answer
a) drive as long as your headlights are used
b) not drive unless you have a mobile phone
c) drive only when your journey is short
d) not drive unless it's essential.

Question 59 (4.30)
When cornering in freezing conditions you should

Mark one answer
a) push the brake down firmly
b) steer with short sharp movements
c) treat the controls of the car gently
d) slow down by braking on the bend

Question 60 (4.42)
How can you tell when you are driving over black ice?

Mark one answer
a) You see black ice on the road
b) The noise from your tyres sounds louder
c) Your steering feels light
d) It is easier to brake

Question 61 (8.33)
You are driving on an icy road. What distance should you drive from the car in front?

Mark one answer
a) Eight times the normal distance.
b) Six times the normal distance.
c) Ten times the normal distance.
d) Four times the normal distance.

Question 62 (8.22)
How should you drive around a bend on ice?

Mark one answer
a) Slowly and smoothly
b) Braking as you enter the bend
c) In first gear
d) Using the clutch and brake together

Question 63 (11.53)
What does this sign mean ?

Mark one answer
a) Multi exit roundabout.
b) Risk of ice.
c) Six road converge.
d) Place of historical interest.

Question 64 (4.57)
Where are you most likely to be affected by a crosswind?

Mark one answer
a) On a busy stretch of road
b) On a long, straight road
c) On an open stretch of road
d) On a narrow country lane

Question 65 (7.27)
Which of these vehicles is LEAST likely to be affected by crosswinds?

Mark one answer
a) Cyclists
b) Cars
c) Motorcyclists
d) High-sided vehicles

Question 66 (7.26)
In which THREE places could a strong crosswind affect your course?

Mark three answers
a) In tunnels
b) On exposed sections of roadway
c) After overtaking a large vehicle
d) When passing gaps in hedges
e) In towns
f) When passing parked vehicles

Question 67 (11.71)
What does this sign mean?

Mark one answer
a) Road noise
b) Adverse camber
c) Crosswinds
d) Airport

Question 68 (4.58)
In windy conditions you need to take extra care when

Mark one answer
a) using the brakes
b) passing pedal cyclists
c) making a hill start
d) turning into a narrow road

Question 69 (1.16)
You see road signs showing a sharp bend ahead. What should you do?

Mark one answer
a) Continue at the same speed.
b) Slow down as you go around the bend.
c) Slow down as you come out of the bend.
d) Slow down before the bend.

Question 70 (11.70)
Which type of vehicle is most affected by strong winds?

Mark one answer
a) Tractor.
b) Motorcycle.
c) Car.
d) Tanker.

Lesson Introduction

The final lesson covers all the theory questions that relate to motorways. The theory on motorways can in some ways be applied in practice using dual carriageways. Consequently, this is why this lesson is undertaken before practical lesson 12 "Dual Carriageways".

Naturally, once you have passed both your theory and driving test it would be wise to take at least a couple of motorway lessons with your driving instructor to minimise the risk of dealing with something you are unfamiliar with.

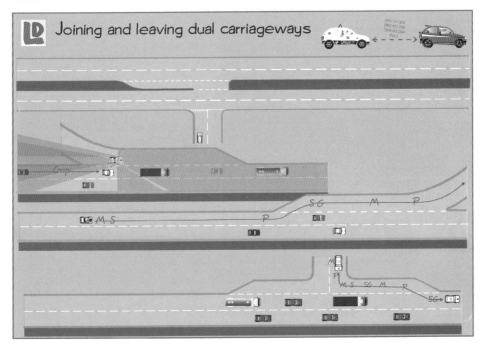

Lesson Study References

Q. 01	Prohibited (HC Rule 155 R 227) (DM Page 215)		Q. 07	Speed Limit (HC Page 53) (DM Page 313)
Q. 02	Maintenance (HC Page 90 TN 60) (DM Page 215)		Q. 08	Normal Driving (HC Rule 164 R 238)
Q. 03	Slip Road (HC Rule 158 R 233) (DM Page 217)			(DM Page 222)
Q. 04	Give way (HC Rule 158 R 233) (DM Page 217)		Q. 09	Crawler Lane (DM Page 222)
Q. 05	Speed Limit (HC Page 53)		Q. 10	Crawler Lane (DM Page 222)
Q. 06	Speed Limit (HC Page 53)		Q. 11	Lane Selection (HC Rule 160 R 233)

Lesson Quiz

Question 1 (9.1)
Which of the following CAN travel on a motorway?

Mark one answer
a) Farm tractors
b) Cyclists
c) Vans
d) Learner drivers

Question 2 (3.57)
You are alone on a motorway and your car has broken down. After telephoning for help you should

Mark one answer
a) accept a lift from a passing motorist
b) remain in a safe place with your vehicle
c) beckon another motorist to stop
d) walk along the motorway to the nearest services.

Question 3 (9.9)
You are joining a motorway. Why is it important to make full use of the slip road?

Mark one answer
a) Because you can continue on the hard shoulder
b) To build up a speed similar to traffic on the motorway
c) To allow you direct access to the overtaking lanes
d) Because there is space available to slow down if you need to

Question 4 (9.11)
When joining a motorway you must always

Mark one answer
a) give way to traffic already on the motorway
b) use the hard shoulder
c) come to a stop before joining the motorway
d) stop at the end of the acceleration lane

Question 5 (9.17)
You are driving a car on a motorway. Unless signs show otherwise you must NOT exceed

Mark one answer
a) 80 mph
b) 60 mph
c) 70 mph
d) 50 mph

Question 6 (9.14)
What is the national speed limit for cars and motorcycles in the centre lane of a three-lane motorway?

Mark one answer
a) 40 mph.
b) 50 mph.
c) 60 mph.
d) 70 mph.

Question 7 (9.16)
You are towing a trailer on a motorway. What is your maximum speed limit?

Mark one answer
a) 40 mph
b) 60 mph
c) 50 mph
d) 70 mph

Question 8 (9.18)
On a three-lane motorway which lane should you use for normal driving

Mark one answer
a) Either right or centre
b) Centre
c) Right
d) Left

Question 9 (9.38)
A crawler lane on a motorway is found

Mark one answer
a) on a steep gradient
b) before a service area
c) before a junction
d) along the hard shoulder

Question 10 (11.94)
What does this sign mean?

Mark one answer
a) Leave motorway at next exit.
b) Lane for heavy and slow vehicles.
c) All lorries use the hard shoulder.
d) Rest area for lorries.

Question 11 (9.12)
You have just joined a motorway. Which lane would you normally stay in to get used to the higher speeds ?

Mark one answer
a) Hard shoulder.
b) Right hand lane.
c) Centre lane.
d) Left hand lane.

Question 12 (9.8)

Immediately after joining a motorway you should normally

Mark one answer
a) try to overtake
b) re-adjust your mirrors
c) position your vehicle in the centre lane
d) keep in the left lane.

Question 13 (9.19)

A basic rule when driving on motorways is

Mark one answer
a) keep to the left lane unless overtaking
b) overtake on the side that is clearest
c) use the lane that has least traffic
d) try to keep above 50 mph to prevent congestion

Question 14 (9.21)

You are driving on a three-lane motorway at 70 mph. There is no traffic ahead. Which lane should you use?

Mark one answer
a) Left lane
b) Right Lane
c) Middle lane
d) Any lane

Question 15 (9.40)

You are travelling in the left-hand lane of a busy motorway. Signs indicate that your lane is closed 800 yards ahead. You should

Mark one answer
a) move over to the lane on your right as soon as it is safe to do so
b) switch on your hazard warning lights and edge over to the lane on your right
c) wait until you reach the obstruction
d) signal right, then pull up and wait for someone to give way

Question 16 (9.22)

The left-hand lane on a three-lane motorway is for use by

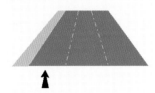

Mark one answer
a) slow vehicles only
b) large vehicles only
c) emergency vehicles only
d) any vehicle

Question 17 (9.23)

The left-hand lane of a motorway should be used for

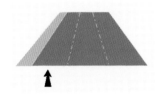

Mark one answer
a) Breakdowns and emergency vehicles only
b) Overtaking slower traffic In the other lanes
c) Slow vehicles only
d) Normal driving

Question 18 (9.25)

Which of the these IS NOT allowed to travel in the right-hand lane of a three-lane motorway?

Mark one answer
a) A small delivery van.
b) A motorcycle.
c) A vehicle towing a trailer.
d) A motorcycle and side-car.

Question 19 (9.24)

What is the right hand-lane used for on a three-lane motorway?

Mark one answer
a) Emergency vehicles only.
b) Overtaking.
c) Vehicles towing trailers.
d) Coaches only.

Question 20 (9.26)

For what reason may you use the right-hand lane of a motorway?

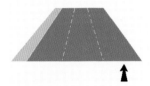

Mark one answer
a) for turning right.
b) for driving at more than 70 mph.
c) for keeping out of the way of lorries.
d) for overtaking other vehicles.

Question 21 (11.149)

The right-hand lane of a three-lane motorway is

Mark one answer
a) for lorries only
b) an overtaking lane
c) the right-turn lane
d) an acceleration lane.

Question 22 (11.140)

Where would you see these road markings?

Mark one answer
a) At a level crossing.
b) On a motorway slip road.
c) At a pedestrian crossing.
d) On a single-track road.

Question 23 (5.46)
You are driving on a road with several lanes. You see these signs above the lanes. What do they mean ?

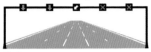

Mark one answer
a) The two right lanes are open.
b) The two left lanes are open.
c) Traffic in the left lanes should stop.
d) Traffic in the right lanes should stop.

Question 24 (6.81)
When driving, ahead of you there is a vehicle with a flashing amber beacon. This means it is

Mark one answer
a) slow moving
b) broken down
c) a doctors car
d) a school crossing patrol

Question 25 (6.101)
As a new driver, how can you decrease your risk of accidents on the motorway?

Mark one answer
a) By taking further training
b) By never driving over 45 mph
c) By driving only in the nearside lane
d) By keeping up with the car in front

Question 26 (9.27)
On motorways you should never overtake on the left UNLESS

Mark one answer
a) you warn drivers behind by signalling left
b) the traffic in the right-hand lane is signalling right
c) there is a queue of traffic to your right that is moving more slowly
d) you can see well ahead that the hard shoulder is clear

Question 27 (9.28)
On a motorway you may ONLY stop on the hard shoulder

Mark one answer
a) if you feel tired and need to rest
b) if you accidentally go past the exit that you wanted to take
c) to pick up a hitchhiker
d) in an emergency

Question 28 (9.36)
What should you use the hard shoulder of a motorway for?

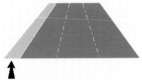

Mark one answer
a) Overtaking
b) Stopping in an emergency
c) Stopping when you are tired
d) Joining the motorway

Question 29 (9.37)
After a breakdown you need to rejoin the main carriageway of a motorway from the hard shoulder. You should

Mark one answer
a) move out onto the carriageway then build up your speed
b) move out onto the carriageway using your hazard lights
c) gain speed on the hard shoulder before moving out onto the carriageway
d) wait on the hard shoulder until someone flashes their headlights at you.

Question 30 (13.65)
On the motorway the hard shoulder should be used

Mark one answer
a) to answer a mobile phone
b) when an emergency arises
c) for a short rest when tired
d) to check a road atlas.

Question 31 (9.31)
You are driving on a motorway. You have to slow down quickly due to a hazard. You should

Mark one answer
a) switch on your hazard lights
b) switch on your headlights
c) sound your horn
d) flash your headlights.

Question 32 (9.33)
You get a puncture on the motorway. You manage to get your vehicle onto the hard shoulder. You should

Mark one answer
a) change the wheel yourself immediately
b) only change the wheel if you have a passenger to help you
c) use the emergency telephone and call for assistance
d) try to wave down another vehicle for help

Question 33 (13.62)
Your vehicle has a puncture on a motorway. What should you do?

Mark one answer
a) Switch on your hazard lights. Stop in your lane
b) Pull up on the hard shoulder. Change the wheel as quickly as possible
c) Drive slowly to the next service area to get assistance
d) Pull up on the hard shoulder. Use the emergency phone to get assistance

Question 34 (13.61)
You are driving on the motorway and get a puncture. You should

Mark one answer
a) pull onto the hard shoulder as safely as possible
b) stop in the lane you are in and change the wheel
c) pull into the central reserve as safely as possible
d) stop in any lane but use emergency flashers

Question 35 (13.67)
You have broken down on a motorway. When you use the emergency telephone you will be asked

Mark three answers
a) for the number on the telephone that you are using
b) for your driving licence details
c) for the name of your vehicle insurance company
d) for details of yourself and your vehicle
e) whether you belong to a motoring organisation

Question 36 (9.35)
How should you use the emergency telephone on a motorway?

Mark one answer
a) Stay close to the carriageway.
b) Face the oncoming traffic.
c) Keep your back to the traffic.
d) Keep your head in the kiosk.

Question 37 (9.34)
The emergency telephones on a motorway are connected to the

Mark one answer
a) ambulance service
b) police control
c) fire brigade
d) braeakdown service

Question 38 (9.15)
What is the national speed limit on motorways for cars and motorcycles ?

Mark one answer
a) 30 mph
b) 50 mph
c) 60 mph
d) 70 mph

Question 39 (9.30)
You are driving on a motorway. The car ahead shows its hazard lights for a short time. This tells you that

Mark one answer
a) the driver wants you to overtake
b) the other car is going to change lanes
c) traffic ahead is slowing or stopping suddenly
d) there is a police speed check up ahead

Question 40 (9.39)
Your vehicle has broken down on a motorway. You are not able to stop on the hard shoulder. What should you do FIRST?

Mark one answer
a) Attempt to repair your vehicle quickly
b) Stop following traffic and ask for help
c) Switch on your hazard warning lights
d) Place a warning triangle in the road

Question 41 (13.72)
You are driving on a motorway. When can you use hazard warning lights?

Mark two answers
a) When a vehicle is following too closely.
b) When you slow down quickly because of danger ahead.
c) When you are towing another vehicle.
d) When driving on the hard shoulder.
e) When you have broken down, on the hard shoulder.

Question 42 (13.64)
You see a car on the hard shoulder of a motorway with a HELP pennant displayed. This means the driver is most likely to be

Mark one answer
a) a disabled person
b) First Aid trained
c) a foreign visitor
d) a rescue patrol person

Question 43 (9.41)
When may you stop on a motorway?

Mark three answers
a) In an emergency or a breakdown
b) When you are tired and need a rest
c) If a child in the car feels ill
d) If red lights show above your lane
e) If you have to read a map
f) When told to by the police

Question 44 (9.43)
You are driving on a motorway There are red flashing lights above every lane. You must

Mark one answer
a) pull onto the hard shoulder
b) leave at the next exit
c) stop and wait
d) slow down and watch for further signals

Question 45 (9.42)
You are allowed to stop on a motorway when you

Mark one answer
a) need to walk and get fresh air
b) wish to pick up hitch hikers
c) are told to do so by flashing red lights
d) need to use a mobile telephone

Question 46 (9.44)
You are driving in the right hand lane on a motorway. You see these overhead signs. This means

Mark one answer
a) move to the left and reduce your speed to 50 mph
b) there are roadwork's 50 metres (55 yards) ahead
c) use the hard shoulder until you've passed the hazard
d) leave the motorway at the next exit

Question 47 (11.143)
What does this motorway sign mean?

Mark one answer
a) Change to the lane on your left
b) Leave the motorway at the next exit
c) Change to the opposite carriageway
d) Pull up on the hard shoulder

Question 48 (11.146)
On a motorway this sign means

Mark one answer
a) Move to the lane on your left
b) Move over onto the hard shoulder
c) Leave the motorway at the next exit
d) Pass a temporary obstruction on the left

Question 49 (11.153)
You see these signs overhead on the motorway. They mean

Mark one answer
a) leave the motorway at the next exit
b) all vehicles use the hard shoulder
c) sharp bend to the left ahead
d) stop, all lanes ahead closed

Question 50 (11.144)
What does this motorway sign mean?

Mark one answer
a) No services for 50 miles
b) Temporary minimum speed 50mph
c) Obstruction 50 meters (165 feet) ahead
d) Temporary maximum speed 50mph

Question 51 (11.145)
What does this sign mean?

Mark one answer
a) 11 tonne weight limit
b) Through traffic use left lane
c) Right-hand lane closed ahead
d) Right-hand lane T-junction only

Question 52 (11.152)
You are travelling along a motorway. You see this sign. You should

Mark one answer
a) leave the motorway at the next exit
b) turn left immediately
c) change lane
d) move onto the hard shoulder.

Question 53 (11.147)
What does '25' mean on this motorway sign?

Mark one answer
a) The distance to the nearest town.
b) The route number of the road.
c) The number of the next junction.
d) The speed limit on the slip road.

Question 54 (11.154)
What does this sign mean?

Mark one answer
a) End of motorway
b) No motor vehicles
c) No through road
d) End of bus lane

Question 55 (9.46)
When driving through a contraflow system on a motorway you should

Mark one answer
a) switch lanes to keep the traffic flowing
b) drive close to the vehicle ahead to reduce queues
c) keep a good distance from the vehicle ahead, for safety
d) ensure that you do not exceed 30 mph for safety

Question 56 (9.47)
You are intending to leave the motorway at the next exit. Before you reach the exit you should normally position your vehicle

Mark one answer
a) in the middle lane
b) in the left-hand lane
c) on the hard shoulder
d) in any lane

Question 57 (9.48)
What do these motorway signs show?

Mark one answer
a) They are countdown markers to the next exit
b) They are distance markers to the next telephone
c) They warn of a police control ahead
d) They are countdown markers to a bridge

Question 58 (9.49)
At night, when leaving a well lit motorway service area, you should

Mark one answer
a) drive for some time using only your sidelights
b) give your eyes time to adjust to the darkness
c) switch on your interior light until your eyes adjust
d) close your eyes for a moment before leaving the slip road.

Question 59 (9.50)
You are driving on a motorway. By mistake, you go past the exit which you wanted to take. You should

Mark one answer
a) carefully reverse on the hard shoulder
b) carefully reverse in the left-hand lane
c) make a U-turn at the next gap in the central reservation
d) carry on to the next exit

Question 60 (9.51)
On a motorway the reflective amber studs can be found between

Mark one answer
a) the hard shoulder and the carriageway
b) the acceleration lane and the carriageway
c) each pair of the lanes
d) the central reservation and the carriageway

Question 61 (9.53)
You are driving on a three-lane motorway. There are red reflective studs on your left and white ones to your right. Where are you?

Mark one answer
a) On the hard shoulder
b) In the left-hand lane
c) In the right-hand lane
d) In the middle lane

Question 62 (9.54)
What colour are the reflective studs
between a motorway and its slip road?

Mark one answer
a)   White
b)   Amber
c)   Red
d)   Green

Question 63 (9.55)
You are travelling on a motorway. What
colour are the reflective studs on the
left of the carriageway?

Mark one answer
a)   Amber
b)   Red
c)   White
d)   Green

Question 64 (11.150)
Where can you find amber studs on a
motorway?

Mark one answer
a)   On the right-hand edge of the
      road
b)   On the left-hand edge of the road
c)   Separating the slip road from the
      motorway
d)   Separating the lanes

Question 65 (11.151)
Where on a motorway would you find
green reflective studs?

Mark one answer
a)   Between the hard shoulder and
      the carriage way
b)   Separating driving lanes
c)   At slip road entrances and exits
d)   Between the carriageway and the
      central reservation

Question 66 (11.148)
You are driving on a motorway. Red
flashing lights appear above your lane.
What should you do?

Mark one answer
a)   Go no further in that lane
b)   Continue in that lane and await
      further information
c)   Stop and wait for an instruction to
      proceed
d)   Drive onto the hard shoulder

Question 67 (11.142)
You are driving on a motorway. There
is a slow-moving vehicle ahead. On the
back you see this sign. You should

Mark one answer
a)   pass on the right
b)   pass on the left
c)   leave at the next exit
d)   drive no further.

Question 68 (13.68)
You are on the motorway. Luggage falls
from your vehicle. What should you
do?

Mark one answer
a)   Pull up on the hard shoulder and
      wave traffic down
b)   Reverse back up the motorway to
      pick it up
c)   Stop at the next emergency
      telephone and contact the police
d)   Stop on the motorway and put on
      hazard lights whilst you pick it up

Question 69 (13.71)
You are driving on a motorway. A large
box falls onto the carriageway from a
lorry ahead of you. The lorry does not
stop. You should

Mark one answer
a)   stop close to the box and switch
      on your hazard warning lights until
      the police arrive
b)   pull over to the hard shoulder,
      then try and remove the box
c)   catch up with the lorry and try to
      get the drivers attention
d)   drive to the next emergency
      telephone and inform the police

Question 70 (13.70)
You are travelling on a motorway.
Asuitcase falls from your vehicle. There
are valuables in the suitcase. What
should you do?

Mark one answer
a)   Reverse your vehicle carefully
      and collect the case as quickly as
      possible.
b)   Stop wherever you are and pick
      up the case but only when there is
      a safe gap.
c)   Stop on the hard shoulder and
      use the emergency telephone to
      inform the police.
d)   Stop on the hard shoulder and
      then retrieve the suitcase
      yourself.

Question 71 (5.37)
What is the first hazard shown in this
picture

Mark one answer
a)   Standing traffic
b)   Oncoming traffic
c)   Junction on the left
d)   Pedestrians

Question 72 (1.25)
On a long motorway journey boredom can cause you to feel sleepy. You should

Mark two answers
a) leave the motorway and find a safe place to stop
b) keep looking around at the surrounding landscape
c) drive faster to complete your journey sooner
d) ensure a supply of fresh air into your vehicle
e) increase the volumn of the car sound system
f) stop on the hard shoulder for a rest.

Question 73 (5.43)
You are driving at 60 mph. As you approach this hazard you should

Mark one answer
a) maintain your speed
b) reduce your speed
c) take the next right turn
d) take the next left turn

Question 74 (5.77)
You are driving along a motorway and become tired. You should

Mark two answers
a) stop at the next service area and rest
b) leave the motorway at the next exit and rest
c) increase your speed and turn up the radio volume
d) close all your windows and set heating to warm
e) pull up on the hard shoulder and change drivers

Question 75 (5.52)
you are driving on a motorway. You feel tired. You should stop

Mark one answer
a) carry on but drive slowly
b) leave the motorway at the next exit
c) complete your journey as quickly as possible
d) stop on the hard shoulder

Question 76 (5.84)
If your motorway jouney seems boring and you feel drowsy whilst driving you should

Mark one answer
a) open a window and drive to the next service area
b) stop on the hard shoulder for a sleep
c) speed up to arrive at your destination sooner
d) slow down and let other drivers overtake

Question 77 (9.29)
You are travelling on a motorway. You decide you need a rest. You should

TWO
Mark one answers
a) stop on the hard shoulder
b) go to service area
c) park on the slip road
d) Park on the central reservation
e) leave at the next exit

Question 78 (10.64)
The dual carriageway you are turning right onto has a narrow central reserve. You should

Mark one answer
a) proceed to central reserve and wait
b) wait until the road is clear in both directions
c) stop in first lane so that other vehicles give way
d) emerge slightly to show your intentions

Question 79 (3.84)
For which TWO of these may you use hazard warning lights

Mark two answer
a) When driving on a motorway, to warn drivers behind of a hazard ahead.
b) When you are double parked on a two-way road.
c) When your direction indicators are not working.
d) When warning oncoming traffic that you intend to stop.
e) When your vehicle has broken down and is causing an obstruction.

Question 80 (3.40)
You are driving on a motorway. The traffic ahead is braking sharply because of an accident. How could you warn following traffic ?

Mark one answer
a) Briefly use the hazard warning lights.
b) Switch on the hazard warning lights continuously.
c) Briefly use the rear fog lights.
d) Switch on the headlamps continuously.

Question 81 (5.19)
You are driving along this dual carriageway. Why may you need to slow down ?

Mark one answer
a) There is a broken white line in the centre.
b) There are solid white lines either side.
c) There are roadworks ahead of you.
d) There are no footpaths.

Question 82 (10.39)
You are driving in the right lane of a dual carriageway. You see signs showing that the right lane is closed 800 yards ahead. You should

Mark one answer
a) move to the left immediately
b) wait and see which lane is moving faster
c) move to the left in good time
d) keep in that lane until you reach the queue

Question 83 (11.90)
What does this sign mean?

Mark one answer
a) The right-hand lane is closed
b) No turning right
c) The right-hand lane ahead is narrow
d) Right-hand lane for buses only

Question 84 (11.91)
What does this sign mean?

Mark one answer
a) Change to the left lane.
b) Leave at the next exit.
c) Contraflow system.
d) One-way street.

Question 85 (11.107)
These flashing red lights mean STOP. In which THREE of the following places could you find them?

Mark three answers
a) Pelican crossings.
b) Lifting bridges.
c) Zebra crossings.
d) Level crossings.
e) Motorway exits.
f) Fire stations.

Question 86 (8.16)
You are driving on the motorway in windy conditions. When passing high-sided vehicles you should

Mark one answer
a) increase your speed
b) be wary of a sudden gust
c) drive alongside very closely
d) expect normal conditions.

Question 87 (9.4)
Which FOUR of these must NOT use motorways?

Mark four answers
a) Learner car drivers.
b) Motorcycles over 50cc.
c) Double-decker busses.
d) Farm tractors.
e) Learner motorcyclists.
f) Cyclists

Question 88 (9.52)
What colour are the reflective studs between the lanes on a motorway?

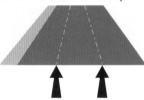

Mark one answer
a) Green.
b) Amber.
c) White.
d) Red.

Lesson Quiz 1

Q	S	Answers	Q	S	Answers	Q	S	Answers
1	1	b	36	1	c	71	2	a, c
2	2	a,c	37	1	c	72	2	c, d
3	1	c	38	3	c, d, e	73	1	c
4	1	c	39	4	a, b, c, e	74	1	d
5	3	c, d, e	40	1	d	75	1	c
6	1	d	41	1	d	76	1	a
7	1	a	42	1	d	77	1	a
8	3	a, b, d	43	1	a	78	1	b
9	3	b, d, e	44	2	b, c	79	1	b
10	3	b, c, f	45	1	d	80	1	d
11	3	b, c, e	46	2	a, b	81	3	a, c, f
12	3	a, b, e	47	3	a, e, f	82	1	a
13	1	b	48	1	b	83	1	d
14	1	b	49	1	a	84	1	a
15	1	a	50	1	d	85	2	a, b
16	1	b	51	1	a	86	1	b
17	1	c	52	1	c	87	1	c
18	1	c	53	2	b, d	88	1	a
19	2	b, d	54	1	d	89	1	b
20	1	a	55	1	b	90	1	b
21	1	d	56	1	c			
22	1	c	57	1	d			
23	2	b, c	58	1	a			
24	1	c	59	1	c			
25	4	a, c, e, f	60	1	a			
26	1	c	61	1	a			
27	1	d	62	2	b, e			
28	3	c, d, e	63	3	d, e, f			
29	3	a, b, f	64	1	a			
30	1	b	65	1	c			
31	2	a, d	66	1	b			
32	2	c, d	67	1	b			
33	3	a, c, e	68	1	a			
34	1	b	69	2	b, c			
35	1	b	70	1	d			

Lesson Quiz 2

Q	S	Answers	Q	S	Answers
1	1	a	36	1	a
2	1	a	37	2	a, e
3	1	b	38	1	d
4	1	a	39	1	c
5	1	d	40	1	d
6	1	a	41	1	a
7	1	d	42	1	b
8	1	b	43	1	b
9	1	a	44	1	a
10	3	b, c, e	45	1	a
11	1	b	46	1	d
12	1	d	47	1	c
13	1	b	48	3	a, d, e
14	1	b	49	1	d
15	1	a	50	1	b
16	1	c	51	1	d
17	1	b	52	4	a, c, e, f
18	1	d	53	1	b
19	1	c	54	2	c, d
20	1	d	55	3	a, b, d
21	1	c	56	1	a
22	1	a	57	1	d
23	1	a	58	1	a
24	1	a	59	1	b
25	1	d	60	1	d
26	1	a	61	1	b
27	1	b	62	1	b
28	1	b	63	1	b
29	1	a	64	1	b
30	1	d	65	1	a
31	1	c	66	1	a
32	2	c, d	67	1	a
33	1	c	68	1	b
34	1	c	69	1	c
35	1	a	70	1	a

Q = Question number S = No. of answers to select

Lesson Quiz 3

Q	S	Answers		Q	S	Answers
1	1	b		36	1	c
2	3	a, c, f		37	1	d
3	1	c		38	1	d
4	2	c, d		39	1	b
5	1	d		40	1	c
6	1	b		41	2	b, c
7	1	d		42	1	b
8	1	b		43	1	a
9	1	c		44	1	d
10	1	b		45	3	d, e, f
11	2	b, d		46	3	a, b, d
12	2	d, f		47	3	a, c, e
13	1	d		48	3	d, e, f
14	1	d		49	1	c
15	1	a, c, e		50	3	a, c, f
16	1	c		51	1	d
17	1	c		52	1	b
18	1	a		53	1	c
19	3	a, c, d		54	1	c
20	1	a		55	1	b
21	1	a		56	3	a, e, f
22	1	d		57	1	b
23	1	b		58	1	b
24	4	a, b, c, d		59	3	b, d, e
25	3	b, d, e		60	1	c
26	3	a, b, d		61	1	b
27	1	c		62	2	a, b
28	1	b		63	2	b, c
29	1	c		64	3	c, d, e
30	4	a, b, c, e		65	1	a
31	1	a		66	4	a, c, d, e
32	2	a, b		67	2	a, e
33	3	a, b, c		68	1	d
34	1	c		69	1	c
35	1	c		70	2	c, d

Lesson Quiz 4

Q	S	Answers		Q	S	Answers
1	1	a		36	1	c
2	1	a		37	1	c
3	1	b		38	1	b
4	1	c		39	1	b
5	1	c		40	1	d
6	1	d		41	1	a
7	1	d		42	1	c
8	1	c		43	1	a
9	1	a		44	1	c
10	1	a		45	1	a
11	1	a		46	1	b
12	1	a		47	1	c
13	1	c		48	1	a
14	1	d		49	1	c
15	1	c		50	1	c
16	3	a, c, d		51	2	d, e
17	3	a, d, e		52	1	a
18	1	a		53	1	a
19	1	d		54	3	d, e, f
20	1	a		55	1	a
21	1	b		56	1	c
22	1	c		57	1	b
23	1	c		58	1	a
24	1	b		59	1	c
25	1	a		60	1	c
26	1	a		61	1	a
27	1	a		62	1	b
28	1	b		63	1	a
29	1	a		64	1	b
30	1	c		65	1	a
31	1	a		66	1	d
32	1	d		67	1	b
33	1	d		68	1	b
34	1	b		69	1	a
35	1	d		70	1	b

Q = Question number   S = No. of answers to select

Lesson Quiz 5

Q	S	Answers		Q	S	Answers
1	1	b		36	1	b
2	3	b, c, d		37	1	c
3	3	a, b, e		38	1	c
4	1	a		39	1	b
5	1	a		40	1	c
6	1	b		41	1	c
7	1	b		42	1	d
8	1	a		43	1	a
9	1	a		44	1	b
10	1	a		45	1	d
11	1	d		46	1	c
12	1	c		47	1	d
13	2	c, e		48	1	a
14	2	a, c		49	3	c, d, e
15	1	c		50	1	b
16	1	c		51	1	b
17	1	d		52	1	d
18	1	a		53	1	b
19	1	a		54	2	c, d
20	1	d		55	1	b
21	1	b		56	1	d
22	1	d		57	1	a
23	1	a		58	1	a
24	3	c, d, e		59	1	a
25	1	d		60	1	b
26	1	d		61	1	a
27	1	a		62	1	a
28	1	c		63	1	c
29	1	c		64	1	a
30	2	b, c		65	1	d
31	2	a, e		66	1	d
32	1	b		67	1	a
33	1	c		68	1	a
34	1	b		69	1	c
35	1	b		70	1	b

Lesson Quiz 6

Q	S	Answers		Q	S	Answers
1	1	a		36	1	a
2	1	d		37	1	d
3	1	b		38	1	b
4	1	d		39	1	d
5	1	b		40	1	c
6	1	c		41	1	a
7	1	d		42	1	c
8	1	d		43	1	d
9	1	d		44	1	b
10	1	b		45	1	b
11	1	a		46	1	c
12	1	c		47	1	c
13	1	a		48	1	c
14	1	b		49	1	a
15	1	b		50	1	c
16	1	d		51	1	a
17	1	a		52	1	c
18	1	d		53	1	d
19	1	c		54	1	c
20	1	b		55	1	a
21	1	b		56	1	a
22	1	d		57	2	a, c
23	1	a		58	1	a
24	1	a		59	1	a
25	1	a		60	3	a, d, f
26	1	b		61	1	d
27	1	b		62	1	b
28	1	b		63	1	b
29	1	a		64	1	a
30	1	a		65	1	b
31	1	c		66	1	c
32	1	b		67	1	d
33	1	c		68	1	b
34	1	d		69	1	a
35	1	b		70	1	d

Q = Question number   S = No. of answers to select

Lesson Quiz 7

Q	S	Answers		Q	S	Answers
1	1	b		36	1	a
2	1	c		37	1	d
3	1	a		38	1	d
4	1	b		39	1	d
5	1	c		40	1	c
6	1	a		41	1	c
7	1	b		42	1	a
8	1	d		43	1	b
9	1	b		44	1	b
10	1	a		45	1	d
11	1	d		46	1	c
12	1	d		47	1	a
13	1	c		48	2	a, c
14	3	a, b, c		49	1	b
15	1	c		50	1	a
16	1	d		51	1	a
17	1	a		52	1	b
18	1	a		53	2	c, d
19	1	b		54	1	a
20	1	d		55	1	a
21	1	b		56	1	c
22	1	d		57	1	c
23	1	c		58	3	a, d, e
24	1	d		59	3	b, d, e
25	1	a		60	1	b
26	3	a, c, e		61	1	c
27	1	b		62	4	c, d, e, f
28	1	a		63	1	a
29	3	a, b, c		64	1	d
30	1	b		65	1	a
31	1	a		66	2	a, d
32	1	a		67	1	b
33	2	c, f		68	1	b
34	1	d		69	1	a
35	1	b		70	1	d

Lesson Quiz 8

Q	S	Answers		Q	S	Answers
1	1	a		36	1	a
2	1	a		37	1	c
3	1	a		38	1	c
4	1	a		39	1	c
5	1	a		40	1	b
6	1	d		41	2	c, d
7	1	c		42	1	d
8	1	d		43	1	b
9	2	b, c		44	1	a
10	1	b		45	1	d
11	1	a		46	1	d
12	1	d		47	1	d
13	1	c		48	1	d
14	1	c		49	1	a
15	1	b		50	1	c
16	1	a		51	1	a
17	1	c		52	1	c
18	1	d		53	1	d
19	1	c		54	3	a, b, d
20	1	c		55	1	c
21	1	b		56	1	a
22	1	a		57	1	c
23	1	a		58	2	a, e
24	1	d		59	1	a
25	1	b		60	1	b
26	1	a		61	2	c, d
27	1	c		62	1	c
28	1	a		63	1	c
29	1	c		64	1	d
30	1	d		65	1	d
31	1	b		66	1	c
32	3	a, c, e		67	1	d
33	1	d		68	1	b
34	3	a, c, d		69	1	d
35	2	a, c		70	1	c

Q = Question number   S = No. of answers to select

Lesson Quiz 9

Q	S	Answers
1	4	a, b, c, d
2	3	a, b, c
3	1	a
4	3	a, b, e
5	1	a
6	2	b, c
7	1	a
8	1	c
9	1	b
10	1	d
11	2	c, d
12	1	d
13	2	a, c
14	1	a
15	1	a
16	1	a
17	3	a, b, c
18	1	a
19	1	d
20	1	b
21	1	a
22	1	a
23	1	b
24	1	a
25	1	d
26	1	c
27	2	a, e
28	1	b
29	1	d
30	1	c
31	1	c
32	1	c
33	1	c
34	1	c
35	1	b

Q	S	Answers
36	2	d, e
37	1	a
38	1	c
39	1	d
40	1	c
41	1	d
42	1	b
43	3	b, d, f
44	2	b, d
45	1	a
46	1	b
47	1	b
48	1	a
49	1	d
50	1	a
51	1	a
52	1	b
53	1	d
54	1	c
55	1	c
56	1	b
57	2	a, b
58	1	c
59	1	d
60	1	b
61	2	a, e
62	1	b
63	1	c
64	1	a
65	1	c
66	1	a
67	1	c
68	3	a, b, d
69	1	a
70	1	a

Lesson Quiz 10

Q	S	Answers
1	2	c, d
2	1	b
3	1	a
4	1	d
5	1	c
6	1	a
7	1	d
8	1	a
9	1	c
10	1	a
11	1	c
12	1	b
13	1	b
14	1	c
15	1	b
16	1	d
17	1	a
18	1	a
19	1	d
20	1	a
21	1	b
22	1	c
23	1	a
24	1	b
25	1	b
26	1	b
27	1	c
28	1	a
29	1	b
30	1	d
31	1	b
32	1	d
33	1	a
34	1	b
35	1	d

Q	S	Answers
36	1	a
37	1	c
38	1	a
39	1	a
40	1	b
41	1	a
42	1	c
43	3	a, c, d
44	1	c
45	1	c
46	1	a
47	1	a
48	1	b
49	1	a
50	1	d
51	1	d
52	1	c
53	1	d
54	1	a
55	1	a
56	1	c
57	1	a
58	1	b
59	2	a, d
60	1	d
61	1	d
62	1	d
63	2	b, d
64	1	a
65	1	a
66	1	a
67	1	a
68	1	b
69	1	d
70	1	b

Q = Question number   S = No. of answers to select

Lesson Quiz 11

Q	S	Answers
1	1	b
2	1	a
3	1	c
4	1	a
5	1	a
6	1	a
7	1	c
8	1	b
9	1	a
10	2	a, b
11	1	c
12	1	c
13	1	b
14	2	a, c
15	1	d
16	1	a
17	1	d
18	1	d
19	1	c
20	1	a
21	1	b
22	1	d
23	1	a
24	1	d
25	1	a
26	2	c, d
27	1	a
28	2	b, d
29	2	a, d
30	1	c
31	1	a
32	1	d
33	1	a
34	4	a, b, d, f
35	1	d

Q	S	Answers
36	1	b
37	3	a, c, e
38	2	a, c
39	1	a
40	1	b
41	1	c
42	1	b
43	1	c
44	1	c
45	1	b
46	1	b
47	1	b
48	1	a
49	1	a
50	1	c
51	1	d
52	1	b
53	1	d
54	1	b
55	4	b, d, e, f
56	1	b
57	1	b
58	1	d
59	1	c
60	1	c
61	1	c
62	1	a
63	1	b
64	1	c
65	1	b
66	3	b, c, d
67	1	c
68	1	b
69	1	d
70	1	b

Lesson Quiz 12

Q	S	Answers
1	1	c
2	1	b
3	1	b
4	1	a
5	1	c
6	1	d
7	1	b
8	1	d
9	1	a
10	1	b
11	1	d
12	1	d
13	1	a
14	1	a
15	1	a
16	1	d
17	1	d
18	1	c
19	1	b
20	1	d
21	1	b
22	1	b
23	1	b
24	1	a
25	1	a
26	1	c
27	1	d
28	1	b
29	1	c
30	1	b
31	1	a
32	1	c
33	1	d
34	1	a
35	3	a, d, e

Q	S	Answers
36	1	b
37	1	b
38	1	d
39	1	c
40	1	c
41	2	b, e
42	1	a
43	1	a, d, f
44	1	c
45	1	c
46	1	a
47	1	a
48	1	a
49	1	a
50	1	d
51	1	c
52	1	a
53	1	c
54	1	a
55	1	c
56	1	b
57	1	a
58	1	b
59	1	d
60	1	d
61	1	b
62	1	d
63	1	b
64	1	a
65	1	c
66	1	a
67	1	b
68	1	c
69	1	d
70	1	c

Q	S	Answers
71	1	c
72	2	a, d
73	1	b
74	2	a, b
75	1	b
76	1	a
77	2	b, e
78	1	b
79	2	a, e
80	1	a
81	1	c
82	1	c
83	1	a
84	1	c
85	3	b, d, f
86	1	b
87	4	a, d, e, f
88	1	c

Q = Question number S = No. of answers to select

136

Question 1
What, according to The Highway Code, do the letters MSM mean?

Mark one answer
a) Mirror, signal, manoeuvre.
b) Manoeuvre, signal, mirror.
c) Mirror, speed, manoeuvre.
d) Manoeuvre, speed, mirror.

Question 2
You have stopped at a pedestrian crossing. To allow pedestrians to cross you should

Mark one answer
a) wait until they have crossed
b) edge your vehicle forward slowly
c) wait, revving your engine
d) signal to pedestrians to cross.

Question 3
You are in a line of traffic. The driver behind you is following very closely. What action should you take?

Mark one answer
a) Slow down, gradually increasing the gap between you and the vehicle in front.
b) Ignore the following driver and continue to drive within the speed limit.
c) Signal left and wave the following driver past.
d) Move out wider to a position just left of the road's centre line.

Question 4
Which THREE does the law require you to keep in good condition?

Mark three answers
a) Gears.
b) Clutch.
c) Headlights.
d) Windscreen.
e) Seat belts.

Question 5
It is illegal to drive with tyres that

Mark one answer
a) have a large deep cut in the side wall
b) have been bought second-hand
c) are of different makes
d) have painted walls.

Question 6
When driving a car fitted with automatic transmission what would you use 'kick down' for?

Mark one answer
a) Cruise control.
b) Quick acceleration.
c) Slow braking.
d) Fuel economy.

Question 7
You wish to park facing DOWNHILL. Which TWO of the following should you do?

Mark two answers
a) Turn the steering wheel towards the kerb.
b) Park close to the bumper of another car.
c) Park with two wheels on the kerb.
d) Put the handbrake on firmly.
e) Turn the steering wheel away from the kerb.

Question 8
The offence of causing death whilst driving under the influence of drink or drugs carries the maximum penalty of

Mark one answer
a) eight years' imprisonment
b) ten years' imprisonment
c) 12 years' imprisonment
d) six years' imprisonment.

Question 9
You are reversing from a driveway and cannot see clearly. There are many pedestrians around. You should

Mark one answer
a) continue whilst sounding your horn
b) continue with your hazard lights on
c) get someone to guide you
d) continue: it is your right of way.

Question 10
What must a driver do at a pelican crossing when the amber light is flashing?

Mark one answer
a) Signal the pedestrian to cross.
b) Always wait for the green light before proceeding.
c) Give way to any pedestrians on the crossing.
d) Wait for the red–and–amber light before proceeding.

Question 11
At toucan crossings

Mark two answers
a) there is no flashing amber light
b) cyclists are not permitted
c) there is a continuously flashing amber beacon
d) pedestrians and cyclists may cross
e) you only stop if someone is waiting to cross.

Question 12
What type of crossing is this?

Mark one answer
a)   A zebra crossing.
b)   A pelican crossing.
c)   A puffin crossing.
d)   A toucan crossing.

Question 13
At night you see a pedestrian wearing reflective clothing and carrying a bright red light. What does this mean?

Mark one answer
a)   You are approaching roadworks.
b)   You are approaching an organised march.
c)   You are approaching a slow-moving vehicle.
d)   You are approaching an accident black spot.

Question 14
You're driving along a road and you see this signal. It means

Mark one answer
a)   cars must stop
b)   trams must stop
c)   both trams and cars must stop
d)   both trams and cars can continue.

Question 15
You are driving in very wet weather. Your vehicle begins to slide. This effect is called

Mark one answer
a)   hosing
b)   weaving
c)   aquaplaning
d)   fading.

Question 16
On a foggy day you unavoidably have to park your car on the road. You should

Mark one answer
a)   leave your headlights on
b)   leave your fog lights on
c)   leave your sidelights on
d)   leave your hazard lights on.

Question 17
What is the right hand-lane used for on a three-lane motorway?

Mark one answer
a)   Emergency vehicles only.
b)   Overtaking.
c)   Vehicles towing trailers.
d)   Coaches only.

Question 18
You are driving on a motorway. The car ahead shows its hazard lights for a short time. This tells you that

Mark one answer
a)   the driver wants you to overtake
b)   the other car is going to change lanes
c)   traffic ahead is slowing or stopping suddenly
d)   there is a police speed check up ahead.

Question 19
There is a tractor ahead of you. You wish to overtake but you are NOT sure if it is safe to do so. You should

Mark one answer
a)   follow another overtaking vehicle through
b)   sound your horn to the slow vehicle to pull over
c)   speed through but flash your lights to oncoming traffic
d)   not overtake if you are in doubt.

Question 20
In which THREE places must you NEVER park your vehicle?

Mark three answers
a)   Near the brow of a hill.
b)   At or near a bus stop.
c)   Where there is no pavement.
d)   Within 10 metres (33 feet) of a junction.
e)   On a 40 mph road.

Question 21
You want to park and you see this sign. On the days and times shown you should

Mark one answer
a)   park in a bay and not pay
b)   park on yellow lines and pay
c)   park on yellow lines and not pay
d)   park in a bay and pay.

Question 22
What is the meaning of this sign?

Mark one answer
a) No entry.
b) Waiting restrictions.
c) National speed limit.
d) School crossing patrol.

Question 23
You are looking for somewhere to park your vehicle. The area is full EXCEPT for spaces marked 'disabled use'. You must

Mark one answer
a) use these spaces when elsewhere is full
b) stay with your vehicle when you park there
c) use these spaces, disabled or not
d) not park there unless permitted.

Question 24
Which sign means no motor vehicles are allowed?

Mark one answer

Sign A

Sign B

Sign C

Sign D

Question 25
What does this sign mean?

Mark one answer
a) New speed limit 20 mph.
b) No vehicles over 30 tonnes.
c) Minimum speed limit 30 mph.
d) End of 20 mph zone.

Question 26
What does this sign mean?

Mark one answer
a) No parking.
b) No road markings.
c) No through road.
d) No entry.

Question 27
What does this sign mean?

Mark one answer
a) Bend to the right.
b) Road on the right closed.
c) No traffic from the right.
d) No right turn.

Question 28
Which sign means 'no entry'?

Mark one answer

Sign A

Sign B

Sign C

Sign D

Question 29
What does this sign mean?

Mark one answer
a) Route for trams only.
b) Route for buses only.
c) Parking for buses only.
d) Parking for trams only.

Question 30
Which type of vehicle does this sign apply to?

Mark one answer
a) Wide vehicles.
b) Long vehicles.
c) High vehicles.
d) Heavy vehicles.

Question 31
What does this sign mean?

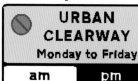

Mark one answer
a) You can park on the days and times shown.
b) No parking on the days and times shown.
c) No parking at all from Monday to Friday.
d) You can park at any time: the urban clearway ends.

Question 32
What does '25' mean on this motorway sign?

Mark one answer
a) The distance to the nearest town.
b) The route number of the road.
c) The number of the next junction.
d) The speed limit on the slip road.

Question 33
The cost of your insurance will be reduced if

Mark one answer
a) your car is large and powerful
b) you are using the car for work purposes
c) you have penalty points on your licence
d) you are over 25 years old.

Question 34
You are in an accident on an 'A' class road. You have a warning triangle with you. At what distance before the obstruction should you place the warning triangle?

Mark one answer
a) 100 metres (330 feet).
b) 45 metres (149 feet).
c) 25 metres (80 feet).
d) 150 metres (492 feet).

Question 35
You are driving on a motorway. When can you use hazard warning lights?

Mark two answers
a) When a vehicle is following too closely.
b) When you slow down quickly because of danger ahead.
c) When you are towing another vehicle.
d) When driving on the hard shoulder.
e) When you have broken down, on the hard shoulder.

Mock Exam 1

Q	S	Answers
1	1	a
2	1	a
3	1	a
4	3	c,d,e
5	1	a
6	1	b
7	2	a,d
8	1	b
9	1	c
10	1	c
11	2	a,d
12	1	d
13	1	b
14	1	b
15	1	c
16	1	c
17	1	b
18	1	c
19	1	d
20	3	a,b,d
21	1	d
22	1	b
23	1	d
24	1	b
25	1	d
26	1	d
27	1	d
28	1	d
29	1	a
30	1	c
31	1	b
32	1	c
33	1	d
34	1	b
35	2	b,e

Question 1
You are driving on a wet road. You have to stop your vehicle in an emergency. You should

Mark one answer
a) apply the handbrake and footbrake together
b) keep both hands on the wheel
c) select reverse gear
d) give an arm signal.

Question 2
You could use the 'Two-Second Rule'

Mark one answer
a) before restarting the engine after it's stalled
b) to keep a safe gap from the vehicle in front
c) before using the 'mirror, signal, manoeuvre' routine
d) when emerging on wet roads.

Question 3
When are you allowed to exceed the maximum speed limit?

Mark one answer
a) Between midnight and 6 am.
b) Never.
c) When overtaking.
d) When the road's clear.

Question 4
New petrol-engined cars must be fitted with catalytic converters. The reason for this is to

Mark one answer
a) control exhaust noise levels
b) prolong the life of the exhaust system
c) allow the exhaust system to be recycled
d) reduce harmful exhaust emissions.

Question 5
Excessive or uneven tyre wear can be caused by faults in the

Mark two answers
a) braking system
b) suspension
c) gearbox
d) exhaust system.

Question 6
You are driving in heavy rain. Your steering suddenly becomes very light. You should

Mark one answer
a) steer towards the side of the road
b) apply gentle acceleration
c) brake firmly to reduce speed
d) ease off the accelerator.

Question 7
You see this sign on the rear of a slow–moving lorry that you want to pass. It is travelling in the middle of the road. You should

Mark one answer
a) cautiously approach the lorry then pass on either side
b) follow the lorry until you can leave the motorway
c) wait on the hard shoulder until the lorry has stopped
d) approach with care and keep to the left of the lorry.

Question 8
You have taken medication that may make you feel drowsy. Your friends tell you it is safe to drive. What should you do?

Mark one answer
a) Take their advice and drive.
b) Ignore your friends' advice and do not drive.
c) Only drive if they come with you.
d) Drive for short distances only.

Question 9
You are driving past parked cars. You notice a wheel of a bicycle sticking out between them. What should you do?

Mark one answer
a) Accelerate past quickly and sound your horn.
b) Slow down and wave the cyclist across.
c) Brake sharply and flash your headlights.
d) Slow down and be prepared to stop for a cyclist.

Question 10
What does this sign tell you?

Mark one answer
a) No cycling.
b) Cycle route ahead.
c) Route for cycles only.
d) End of cycle route.

Question 11
Where would you see this sign?

Mark one answer
a) In the window of a car taking children to school.
b) At the side of the road.
c) At playground areas.
d) On the rear of a school bus or coach.

Question 12
Where would you see this sign?

Mark one answer
a) On the approach to a school crossing.
b) At a playground entrance.
c) On a school bus.
d) At a 'pedestrians only' area.

Question 13
A pedestrian steps out into the road just ahead of you. What should you do FIRST?

Mark one answer
a) Sound your horn.
b) Check your mirror.
c) Flash your headlights.
d) Press the brake.

Question 14
You are travelling behind a bus that pulls up at a bus stop. What should you do?

Mark two answers
a) Accelerate past the bus sounding your horn.
b) Watch carefully for pedestrians.
c) Be ready to give way to the bus.
d) Pull in closely behind the bus.

Question 15
You are driving in poor visibility. You can see more than 100 metres (330 feet) ahead. How can you make sure that other drivers can see you?

Mark one answer
a) Turn on your dipped headlights.
b) Follow the vehicle in front closely.
c) Turn on your rear fog lights.
d) Keep well out towards the middle of the road.

Question 16
You are driving at night. Why should you be extra careful of your speed?

Mark one answer
a) Because you might need to stop within the distance that you can see.
b) Because it uses more petrol.
c) Because driving with the lights on runs down the battery.
d) Because you may be late.

Question 17
You are driving on a motorway. You have to slow down quickly due to a hazard. You should

Mark one answer
a) switch on your hazard lights
b) switch on your headlights
c) sound your horn
d) flash your headlights.

Question 18
Which vehicles are normally fitted with amber flashing beacons on the roof?

Mark two answers
a) Doctor's car.
b) Bomb disposal team.
c) Blood transfusion team.
d) Breakdown recovery vehicles.
e) Coastguard.
f) Maintenance vehicles.

Question 19
You park overnight on a road with a 40 mph speed limit. You should

Mark one answer
a) park facing the traffic
b) park with sidelights on
c) park with dipped headlights on
d) park near a street light.

Question 20
You can park on the right-hand side of a road at night

Mark one answer
a) in a one-way street
b) with your sidelights on
c) more than 10 metres (33 feet) from a junction
d) under a lamp-post.

Question 21
You are driving at night with full beam headlights on. A vehicle is overtaking you. You should dip your lights

Mark one answer
a) some time after the vehicle has passed you
b) before the vehicle starts to pass you
c) only if the other driver dips his headlights
d) as soon as the vehicle passes you.

Question 22
You are entering an area of roadworks. There is a temporary speed limit displayed. You must

Mark one answer
a) not exceed the speed limit
b) obey the limit only during rush hour
c) accept the speed limit as advisable
d) obey the limit except for overnight.

Question 23
While driving, you approach roadworks. You see a temporary maximum speed limit sign. You must

Mark one answer
a) comply with the sign during the working day
b) comply with the sign at all times
c) comply with the sign when the lanes are narrow
d) comply with the sign during the hours of darkness.

Question 24
What does this sign mean?

Mark one answer
a) End of restricted speed area.
b) End of restricted parking area.
c) End of clearway.
d) End of cycle route.

Question 25
Which sign means 'no stopping'?

Mark one answer

Sign A

Sign B

Sign C

Sign D

Question 26
What does this sign mean?

Mark one answer
a) Roundabout.
b) Crossroads.
c) No stopping.
d) No entry.

Question 27
What does this sign mean?

Mark one answer
a) Distance to parking place ahead.
b) Distance to public telephone ahead.
c) Distance to public house ahead.
d) Distance to passing place ahead.

Question 28
What does this sign mean?

Mark one answer
a) Vehicles may not park on the verge or footway.
b) Vehicles may park on the left-hand side of the road only.
c) Vehicles may park fully on the verge or footway.
d) Vehicles may park on the right-hand side of the road only.

Question 29
Which sign means 'traffic has priority over oncoming vehicles'?

Mark one answer

Sign A

Sign B

Sign C

Sign D

Question 30
What shape is a stop sign at a junction?

Mark one answer

Sign A

Sign B

Sign C

Sign D

Question 31

Which shape of traffic sign means that you must stop?

Mark one answer

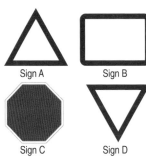

Sign A   Sign B

Sign C   Sign D

Question 32

The right-hand lane of a three-lane motorway is

Mark one answer

a) for lorries only
b) an overtaking lane
c) the right-turn lane
d) an acceleration lane.

Question 33

An MOT certificate is normally valid for

Mark one answer

a) three years after the date it was issued
b) 10,000 miles
c) one year after the date it was issued
d) 30,000 miles.

Question 34

Your car is fitted with child safety door locks. When used this means that normally

Mark one answer

a) the rear doors can only be opened from the outside
b) the rear doors can only be opened from the inside
c) all the doors can only be opened from the outside
d) all the doors can only be opened from the inside.

Question 35

Your vehicle is fitted with child safety door locks. You should use these so that children inside the car cannot open.

Mark one answer

a) the right-hand doors
b) the left-hand doors
c) the rear doors
d) any of the doors.

Mock Exam 2

Q	S	Answers
1	1	b
2	1	b
3	1	b
4	1	d
5	2	a,b
6	1	d
7	1	d
8	1	b
9	1	d
10	1	b
11	1	d
12	1	c
13	1	d
14	2	b,c
15	1	a
16	1	a
17	1	a
18	2	d,f
19	1	b
20	1	a
21	1	d
22	1	a
23	1	b
24	1	b
25	1	b
26	1	c
27	1	a
28	1	c
29	1	c
30	1	d
31	1	c
32	1	b
33	1	c
34	1	a
35	1	c